# INSIGHT POCKET GUIDES

# COSTADELSOL

*Spain's Southern Coast*

GW00726950

PUBLICATIONS

*Dear Visitor!*

**M**arbella is the queen of Europe's holiday destinations, presiding over a string of other well-known resorts along the Costa del Sol and offering easy access to magnificent sierras and southern Andalusia's Moorish cities.

In these pages Insight Guides' correspondent on the Costa del Sol, Barnard Collings, has devised a range of itineraries to bring you the best of this beautiful region, combining lazy days on the best beaches with drives through some of Spain's loveliest scenery to monumental cities and perched 'pueblos'. Using Marbella as a springboard (though any of the other resorts will serve as well), he has devised five full-day itineraries for visitors planning to stay for a week or less; these are followed by 12 optional itineraries and excursions providing detailed suggestions for active holidaymakers with more time. All itineraries include recommended stops for rest and refreshment

**Barnard Collings** has lived in Marbella for the last 18 years. He first visited the region with friends when he was in his mid-twenties. While his companions threw themselves into infiltrating Marbella's high society, he set off to explore the hinterland. Today, Collings is as fond as anyone of the pleasures the Costa offers, especially its many fine restaurants, but he retains his passion for plunging off the beaten track to discover, for himself, and for his friends, the quintessential Spain.

*Hans Höfer*
*Publisher, Insight Guides*

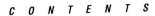
## History & Culture

From the flowering and decline of Moorish Andalusia
to the region's rebirth as one of Europe's leading
holiday destinations – a concise introduction to the
rich history and culture of the Costa del Sol..................**10–17**

## Marbella and the Costa del Sol's Highlights

**Five full-day tours concentrating on the area's chief
pleasures and attractions.**

**Day 1** focuses on *Marbella*, in particular the *Old
Town*. Afterwards a drive to *Benahavís* for lunch. On
the way back, a stop at *Puerto Banús*, the Costa's most
famous marina. The evening includes dinner at a top
restaurant and flamenco until the early hours......................**21**

**Day 2 Málaga** travels east of Marbella to the
province's capital, an historic city often overlooked by
tourists. A tour of the town includes the impressive
*Cathedral* and the *Alcazaba*. The return journey to
Marbella takes a detour to *Mijas* .........................................**26**

**Day 3 Ronda** is a scenic drive to one of Spain's most
spectacularly sited towns. It takes in fine palaces,
churches and museums; the ruins of Arab baths; and
one of the oldest bullrings in Spain......................................**32**

**Day 4 Antequera** is a day's excursion to another
historic city, crammed with notable churches and
Moorish remains. The emphasis is on architecture,
but the afternoon includes a walk through the *Parque
Natural El Torcal de Antequera* .............................................**38**

**Day 5 A Day of Indulgence** concentrates on the
pleasures offered by Marbella's beach clubs .........................**43**

## Pick & Mix Itineraries

**Twelve more itineraries, this time catering to a
variety of time frames and tastes. Some are
extensions of routes covered in the Day Itineraries
section; others are short tours from Marbella.**

**1 Morning or Afternoon in Istàn** is an easy drive
into the spectacular countryside just behind Marbella..........**46**

**2 Lunch at the Refugio de Juanar** is a short
drive to a secluded inn for lunch. Afterwards, a walk
along the forested trails of the *Sierra Blanca* ......................**49**

**3 Morning in Estepona** investigates Marbella's
coastal neighbour, *Estepona*, and then takes a
leisurely drive into the *Sierra Bermeja*..................................**49**

**4 Morning or Afternoon in Casares** is a lovely
drive to one of the Costa's least spoilt yet most
photographed *pueblos* .........................................................**51**

*Pages 2/3:
a perfect location*

**5  Gaucín, Castellar, Sotogrande** extends
Itinerary No 4 to *Gaucín* and *Jimena de la Frontera*,
both topped by Moorish castles. Returning to the
coast, it stops off at *Puerto de Sotogrande*...........................**53**

**6  Ardales, Lakes, El Chorro** is a day's drive
punctuated by *pueblos*, Moorish castles and lakes. It
culminates at *El Chorro* gorge ..............................................**54**

**7  La Axarquìa, Nerja, Frigiliana** explores the
coast east of Marbella and Málaga, in particular the
resort of *Nerja*, with its famous caves....................................**57**

**8  Torremolinos** samples the evening pleasures of
the Costa's notorious 'good-time' resort................................**60**

**9  Café Royale and Fortuna Night Club**  spends
an evening in *Fuengirola*........................................................**62**

## Excursions

Three excursions for visitors with more time.

**10  Sierra Villages, Fresh Trout and Caves**
explores the spectacular region surrounding *Ronda*, in
particular the villages *Grazalema* and *El Bosque* ..................**64**

**11  Roman Arcos, Traditional Villages and
Windsurfing** is an extension of Itinerary No 10,
swooping into Cadiz province before returning to
the coast near *Tarifa*, beloved of windsurfers.........................**67**

**12  Spa Cure, Salt Lake and Parador** is an
extension of Itinerary No 6, exploring the towns and
lakes north of *Ardales* and then curling round to
*Antequera*, where it suggests an overnight stop ...................**72**

*Pages 8/9:
Andalusian
'white town'*

## Shopping & Dining

Tips on what to buy and where to dine ..........................**74–81**

## Calendar of Events

A month by month list of all the main festivals ................**82–3**

## Practical Information

All the background information you may need for your
stay. Includes a list of hand-picked hotels .....................**84–92**

## Maps

| | | | |
|---|---|---|---|
| **Spain** | ......................4 | **Málaga** | ................................26 |
| **The Costa del Sol** | ........18–19 | **Ronda** | .................................32 |
| **Discovering Marbella** | .......21 | **Antequera** | ...........................38 |

*Index and Credits 94–7*

# HISTORY

## Prehistoric Painters and Greeks Bearing Gifts

The first visitors to the coast of southeastern Spain settled some 22 millennia ago. Cave paintings, dating from 20,000 to 15,000BC, show that Palaeolithic man had arrived. Skeletons, artefacts and sanctuary sites located both along the coast and inland speak of an important prehistoric culture here. Some 4,000 years ago in Antequera, a people about whom little is known demonstrated the ability to move huge stone slabs known as dolmens, weighing up to 180 tons each, across great distances, accurately moving them into position to build cave tombs. After these early engineers and artists came the Phoenicians, the Greeks and the Carthaginians.

Large tracts of the Andalusian countryside are covered with olives and vines, gifts of the Phocaean Greeks, who established trading posts

*Antequera, site of prehistoric dolmens*

# Culture

*Antequera's Iglesia San José*

along the coastline after 1000BC. Five hundred years later, the Phoenicians established the settlement of Malaca (Málaga), their second most important trading post along Iberia's shores. It was they who laid the foundations of the city's castle. After the Phoenicians' influence waned in the Mediterranean, Carthage, their offshoot state in North Africa, ousted the Greeks from the coast, moving inland as well, though not much evidence remains of the Carthaginians' presence. Between 264 and 241BC, in their first confrontation with Rome for dominance, they lost nearly all their Iberian colonies and, by the end of the Second Punic War (219–201BC), their power base on the peninsula was destroyed.

## Roman Andalusia

Rome began to build energetically – an unarguable demonstration of its dominance and the physical imposition of its centralised rule over the new province. Hispania Ulterior, part of which was later renamed Baetica, corresponded to today's Andalusia. Corduba (Córdoba), its administrative capital, became the largest and richest city on the peninsula. The Via Augusta was built to connect Rome with Cádiz and today's N340 coastal highway closely follows its line. Improvements in infrastructure included aqueducts such as the one to be seen in Nerja; a theatre in Málaga is an example of the Romans' grand public structures. Finds in the vicinity of Marbella – some of which can be seen in the town's museum – suggest that the Romans were in place here in the 1st century BC and that Marbella may have been the site of their settlement named Silniana.

Near the beach of San Pedro de Alcántara there are remnants of a bathhouse which was part of a larger complex, and ruins of a Roman villa remain at the mouth of the Río Verde. Baetica was where Julius Caesar and Pompey executed the final moves in their competition for supremacy. Emperors Trajan and Hadrian, the philosopher Seneca, writers Lucan and Martial, and Ossius, originator of the Nicene Creed, were among famous locally-born Romans. Hispano-Romans spoke a language and lived by legal codes which formed the basis for those used in Spain today. By the year 400, Christianity was the state religion and the Roman Empire was in decline. In Baetica, which had been made a productive agricultural region, a self-indulgent ruling class was enjoying the high life in towns and on their *latifundias* (extensive estates) worked by slaves.

## Christian Visigoths and Muslim Invaders

Germanic Visigoths, adherents of the Aryan Christianity of Byzantium, arrived on the peninsula as allies of Rome but encountered little opposition when in 468 they claimed Rome's provinces for themselves. The Hispano-Roman nobility identified with the Visigothic

aristocracy, a top-heavy institution in constant dispute over the election of kings — 33 in the 297 years of their rule on the peninsula. The local form of Latin, and much of Roman law, was adopted by the Visigoths who in 590 also made Christianity their state religion. High-level intrigues, from which the Church was not excluded, encouraged the Muslim invasion from North Africa in 711. Evidence of Visigothic supremacy in the region is limited, but they were the originators of the horseshoe arch widely adopted by later Moorish builders.

Some 50,000 Moors, diverse factions united by their Muslim religion, arrived on the peninsula after the initial invasion and victory over the Visigothic army near Gibraltar. Berbers were in the majority but Arabs provided the leadership, administration, language, culture and aristocracy. Most of the disaffected majority under Visigothic rule, as well as the Jews, welcomed the

*Moorish craftsmanship*

Moors, who rapidly took control of the peninsula except for the northwest and the Basque country where Christian resistance was greatest. Al-Andalus was the name they gave their new territory.

Meanwhile in Damascus, the ruling Omayyad dynasty was overthrown. Its only survivor made his way to al-Andalus and in 756 established himself as Abd-al-Rahman I, an independent emir with Córdoba as his capital. He sought to unite the factions and began building a state in which there was religious tolerance and generous patronage of learning and culture. In many places the Moors

**12**

built on what had been there before. Málaga's *alcazar* has examples of horseshoe arches, which the Moors supported on Roman columns and capitals. Stones from what may have been a Roman temple were used to build the *alcázar* of Marbelah (or Marbillia) during the 10th century. Today's streets of Peral, Solano, Arte, Muro and Tetuán follow the line of the original Moorish walls which were punctuated by defensive towers and three gates.

## Divided and Conquered

Politically all was not well in al-Andalus when Abd-al-Rahman III came to power. He settled the internal dissension and undertook campaigns against the Christians nibbling at his northern borders. Then, in 929, feeling secure, he declared himself Caliph, independent of the Eastern Caliphate.

## The Moorish Ethic

It is what happened in southern Iberia before the unification of Christian Spain which most distinguishes Andalusia from the rest of the country. And of most significance is the long Moorish presence in the region: it is some 500 years since the reconquest of Marbella but the Moors ruled it for almost 775 years. Moorish Spain was a cultured Athens compared with the spartan Christian kingdoms. In al-Andalus learning and beauty were admired; a silky life of wine, women and song was the ideal. More important in Castile and the other kingdoms were the horsehair shirt and a demonstration of hard work, military prowess, statecraft and religious zeal. An Andalusian is still more likely to put off work until *mañana* if there's pleasure to be had today, and more likely to admire poets than politicians or priests. The Andalusian's cavalier attitude to time, male *machismo* and indulgence of children are reflected in today's Arab societies.

Muslim al-Andalus was reaching the height of its glory. In the West, Córdoba had no equal as a city, in size, splendour, culture and learning. Hakam II continued the enlightened and effective rule of his father but, as with the Romans and Visigoths before, the upper classes were losing interest in most things but their privilege and pleasure, and the masses were increasingly discontented.

During most of the reign of weak Hisham II, the militarist Almansur was the Caliphate's effective ruler. He imposed civic discipline, initiated public works and effectively campaigned against the Christian kingdoms, ransacking Barcelona, León and the pilgrimage city of Santiago de Compostela. Following his death, the Caliphate sank into disarray and in 1031 it was abolished. Along largely racial lines, Muslim Spain divided into 26 small kingdoms called *taifas*. This cultural division goes some way to explain the differences among people and their customs encountered in Andalusia today. Sevilla, the most dominant kingdom, was a stronghold of *Andalusíes*, Muslims of Arab or Spanish descent born in al-Andalus. Málaga, Marbella, much of the south coast and Antequera were to become part of the kingdom of Granada, a Berber bastion of the Moorish presence in al-Andalus for another 460 years.

Some *taifas* found security in becoming vassals of Christian kingdoms which, inspired by their increasing mutual co-operation, Muslim disunity and an injection of religious zeal, stepped up the momentum of their Reconquest. After Toledo fell to Christian forces in 1085, Sevilla and other *taifas* summoned the help of the Al-moravides, a puritanical sect in North Africa, who arrived, beat back the Christians and decided to stay on in al-Andalus, which they progressively subjugated. Their harsh rule soon proved odious to free-thinking Muslims, and terrifying for Christians and Jews. Sixty years later, the Almohades, a more tolerant sect, ousted their North African rivals and in al-Andalus a new collection of *taifas* filled the power vacuum. The Almohades began reuniting the rival kingdoms, reviving the troubled economy, encouraging scholarship and raising fine buildings of which Seville's Giralda tower is a glorious example.

## The Reconquest and the Road to Unity

The Christian victory at the battle of Las Navas de Tolosa in 1212 tolled the death knell for the Almohades and signalled the end of Muslim sway in al-Andalus as, one after another, their major centres fell to Christian forces. Huge churches, such as Seville's cathedral, were built to glorify and consolidate the faith. Soon only the Moorish kingdom of Granada remained. For nearly 250 years its Nasrid dynasty maintained independent rule through skilful alliances and an effective defence of its borders. The Nasrids began building the Alhambra fortress palace which by 1390 Mohamed V had polished into the architectural delight we marvel at now. Much of the rest of al-Andalus was parcelled out to Christian knights. Some were honoured with titles and very large *latifundias*, harking back to the land division of Roman times and laying the groundwork for agrarian neglect and social injustice which has persisted through the centuries. Many Muslims sought refuge in Granada. Those who stayed in Christian territory, *mudéjares*, worked as artisans, craftsmen and agricultural labourers but, as with the Jews, who served in the professions, it was impossible for them to move up the social ladder without incurring the wrath of Christian citizens.

Following their marriage in

### The 'Mudéjar' Legacy

Systems of water management still in use today and the introduction of new crops, fruits and herbs are significant legacies of the Moors. Fine Moorish architecture is most grandly on show in the magnificent Mezquita of Córdoba and Granada's glorious Alhambra. In buildings which followed in Gothic, Renaissance and baroque styles it is often the addition of delicate *mudéjar* craftsmanship in ceramic, wood and stucco which is the most notable feature. Moorish domestic architecture has persisted over centuries and is now adapted to fill the needs of modern urban builders: cube houses in clustered villages resemble Berber communities in North Africa; the Roman *atrium* serves as a central patio providing privacy, shade, colour and bubbling water; narrow streets predominate, from which buildings exclude the hot sun.

1469, Ferdinand of Aragón and Isabella of Castile, *los Reyes Católi-cos*, ruled Christian Spain in partnership. In 1485 their forces captured Marbella; after a long seige, Málaga succumbed two years later; Boabdil, the last Nasrid king, surrendered Granada in January 1492. The Reconquest was complete. Subsequent persecution and banishment of Muslims and Jews, the most accomplished agriculturists and administrators, gravely damaged the region's economy. It was also in 1492 that Cristóbal Colón – Christopher Columbus – sailed from Andalusia and first landed in the Americas. Spain's economic concentration began to be directed westward. Much of the wealth shipped back was expended in an explosion of grand building. The cathedrals of Málaga and Granada are examples of great religious buildings constructed at the time. Palaces and churches in towns like Ronda and Antequera are other reminders of this building spree. In Marbella, the fortifications were strengthened and much of the street plan of today's Old Town was determined by the mid-16th century, when there were some 800 houses in the municipal area.

## Andalusia's Day in the Sun

But beyond grandiose buildings, Andalusia benefited little from Columbus's 'discovery' of the New World and Spain's subsequent position as the world's richest and most powerful nation. For centuries, no matter who ruled in Madrid, neglect, stagnation and poverty were the rule on the coast. A new invasion brought relief. From the late 1950s onward, an emergent holiday industry began delivering sun-starved Europeans in ever increasing numbers. Building and catering for these foreigners have become the region's biggest economic activities. A strip city stretches laterally more than 150km (93 miles) west from Málaga. Land sales and development continue, spreading further and further inland. Andalusia's south coast has ex-

*A modern tourist villa development*

## The 'Cinderella' Resort

Marbella had a rudimentary economy based on smallholdings, fishing and iron mining when in the early 1950s a marquis, Don Ricardo Soriano, opened some chalets and a *venta* in the area of El Fuerte. Wealthy friends and family came to stay, including his nephew, Prince Alfonso von Hohenlohe of Liechtenstein. The prince bought a fig plantation and *cortijo* which he transformed and opened as the Marbella Club in 1953. It set the tone for Marbella's development as a more exclusive, higher-priced holiday resort and residential area. Other centres along the Costa del Sol opted to serve the mass market and are regretting it.

perienced a new European phenomenon – the mass emigration to the sun of retired people. The invasion of holidaymakers and expatriate residents is a mixed blessing, however, threatening the Costa del Sol's environment and traditional way of life, while securing material security for the local people. During the quincentenary celebrations of Columbus's first voyage and its hosting of Expo '92, Andalusia received a further massive injection of investment.

The extended family remains a strong social force in Andalusia. Almost as important is loyalty to the local community and membership of a tight circle of friends. It is not easy to get to know Andalusians and it is best to make the attempt when they are happy – *not* when they are serving you. Being waiters or shop assistants is not what they aspire to: men tend to see themselves as matadors, flamenco dancers and strutting Don Juans; women first want to be demure virgins, then fussing mothers adored by beautiful, finely-dressed children.

These are all stereotypes, of course, and there are very many exceptions in a rapidly changing society. It is too early to see with what values the post-Franco generations, exposed to all the influences of modern society, are going to enter middle age. The majority of their parents have recent memories of poverty and strong ties to the land. Their religion has little to do with intricate Catholic theology, but offers simple explanations, hope and redemption centred on the veneration of the Virgin Mary.

*Children are the centre of family life*

# Historical Outline

**20,000–1,000BC** Prehistoric cave-dwellers populate south-eastern Spain; Iberians arrive from North Africa. Mining becomes important in the Bronze Age; near Huelva the fabulously rich state of Tartessos is founded. Phoenicians come to trade, introducing the concepts of writing and money.

**500** Carthaginians displace the Greeks, and ravage Tartessos.

**201** Rome wins Second Punic War and consolidates its sovereignty throughout the Iberian peninsula.

**1st century AD** Roman Baetica, with Córdoba as its capital, contributes munificently to the empire's food supply and wealth.

**400** Roman Empire in rapid decline; Germanic tribes invade the peninsula. Vandals reach the south and are chased into North Africa by the Visigoths, Rome's allies.

**475** Rome concedes Visigothic rule in its Iberian provinces.

**711** King Roderick defeated by treachery and a Muslim force from North Africa led by Tarik.

**756** Abd-al-Rahman I founds the Omayyad dynasty in Córdoba and becomes the first ruler of Muslim al-Andalus.

**929** Abd-al-Rahman III proclaims an independent Caliphate; al-Andalus reaching its zenith.

**1212** The defeat at Las Navas de Tolosa is decisive in the decline of Muslim power.

**1492** Christian Spain's *annus mirabilis*: Granada, last Muslim kingdom, falls; Columbus reaches America; Jews are banished.

**1600** Much of Spain's wealth drained by Carlos V and Felipe II in European territorial struggles and fighting the Reformation; culturally Spain is entering its Golden Age. Cervantes and Lope de Vega are writing; the Andalusians Velázquez and Murillo are painting; baroque is the style of Cano and other architects.

**1700** Spain's last Hapsburg king dies; Europe is plunged into the War of the Spanish Succession. The Bourbon Felipe V wins. Two wars with Britain mark the century.

**1808–14** During the War of Independence, Napoleon's armies help themselves to art treasures.

**1900** Spain has lost all its colonies. Reform movements in Andalusia are ruthlessly subdued.

**1931** After permitting the dictator Primo de Rivera to run the country for seven years, Alfonso XIII flees the country and a republic is declared.

**1936** A National Front government fails to stem political chaos. General Franco assumes leadership of an uprising to which Hitler and Mussolini lend support.

**1939** End of horrific Civil War; Franco supreme.

**1953** The United States concludes a defence pact with Franco; the country's low costs and sun begin to attract more tourists.

**1975** King Juan Carlos I begins shepherding the country towards democracy and into the European fold; economic progress and a spectacular cultural revival.

**1982** Socialist Felipe González heads the government.

**1991** A maverick independent candidate Jesús Gil sweeps the board in Marbella's mayoral elections, ushering in a new optimism.

**1992** Seville hosts Expo '92.

**Winter 1995–6** Four years of devastating drought in Southern Spain come to an end.

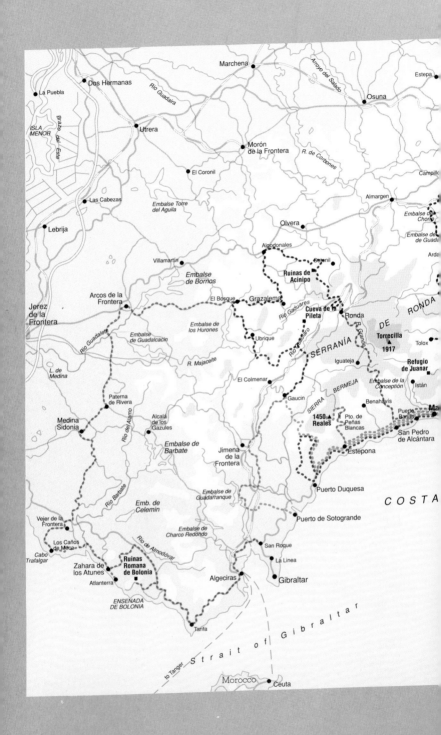

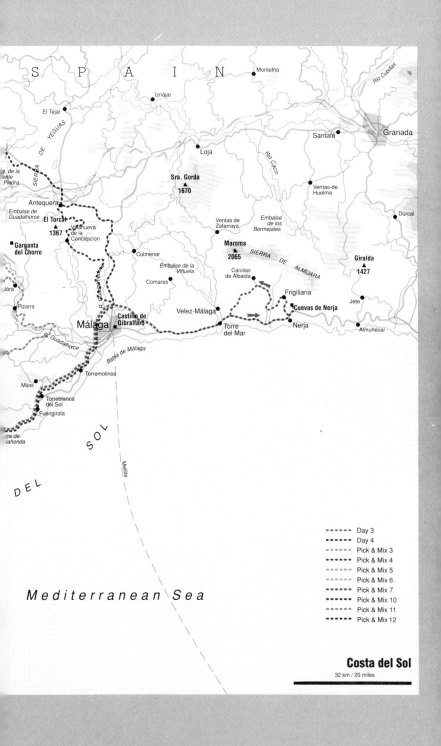

Costa del Sol

32 km / 20 miles

# Day Itiner

In designing *Insight Pocket Guide: Marbella and the Costa del Sol*, we have assumed that you will be visiting the area for a stay of about a week and based in Marbella (though itineraries can easily be adapted for holidaymakers staying in any of the other coastal resorts), you will have come for more than sun and sea, and be willing and ready to explore further afield and in-

land with the aid of a hire car (see *Practical Information, page 88,* for advice on car hire and motoring hints).

The first five Day Itineraries in this guide will introduce you to Marbella town and its surroundings, take you to the underrated port city and provincial capital of Málaga, and to the monumental inland towns of Ronda and Antequera. You will visit world-famous as well as little-known marina developments, both traditional, backwater villages and those that have been smartened up to foreign tastes, and drive through glorious countryside to take in impressive natural as well as man-made sights.

Day 5, which is one of total relaxation and indulgence, allows you time to reflect on all you have seen, and if your stay is longer, you will probably want to repeat this dose of sheer relaxation. This is followed by 14 optional morning, afternoon and evening itineraries, and three excursions from which you may like to pick and mix, all of them packed with suggestions for many other places to see and things to do. Each itinerary contains suggestions on where to eat and drink and, where appropriate, spend the night.

If you wish to travel further afield, to Andalusia's great Morrish cities of Granada, Córdoba and Seville, you are advised to obtain *Insight Pocket Guide: Seville, Córdoba & Granada* which gives these cities the detailed attention they so richly deserve.

## DAY 1

### Discovering Marbella

A leisurely investigation through Marbella town; then by car to the village of Benahavís, where lunch can be simple and inexpensive; a look at Marbella's little sister, San Pedro de Alcántara, and a visit to the famed 'pueblo' marina of Puerto Banús; an evening in Marbella's Old Town, with a fine dinner and a flamenco 'tablao'.

If you want to dine in style tonight, before setting off call Restaurante La Fonda (tel: 277 2512) and reserve a table for 10pm.

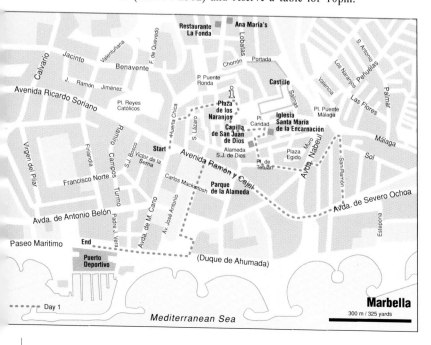

*Awaiting custom*

To reach the heart of the Old Town from Marbella's central spine, Avenida Ramón y Cajal, turn up Calle Huerta Chica, then turn right to enter tiny Plaza de Victoria and exit on the right via Calle de la Estación into **Plaza de los Naranjos** (Orange Tree Square). This is the gathering place of Marbella Old Town. Before taking a table inside or outside at one of the bars, all much the same and all relatively over-priced, call in at the Municipal Tourist Office, occupying part of the **Casa Consitorial** or **Ayuntamiento** (Town Hall) and ask if you may have the following free maps, plans, and booklets: *Marbella Termino Municipal Mapa y Guía*; *Marbella Casco Urbano Plano*; *Costa del Sol Occidental Guía Practica*; *Andalucía Mapa Turistico*, and the *Costa del Sol What's On*, a useful monthly guide. Thus armed, peruse them over a *cafe con leche* in the square.

Also on the *plaza* is the **Casa del Corregidor** (Chief Magistrate's House), completed in 1552, which has a notable stone portico in Gothic-*mudéjar* style, an attractive iron balcony in front of a pointed arch and a Renaissance gallery above. The Renaissance fountain dates from 1504; very recent is the bust of King Juan Carlos I. The unadorned **Ermita de Santiago** (labelled Cofradia del S. Cristo del Amor), which dates from the 15th century, sits unassumingly on the southwest corner.

Map in hand, wander around the Old Town at will for an hour. Concentrate on the maze of alleys within the perimeter of Avenida Ramón y Cajal, and *calles* Huerta Chica, Peral, Solano, Portada, Arte and Avenida Nabeul. You will note shops, bars and eating places to which you may want to return tonight or later. Bars

*Plaza de los Naranjos*

range from the highly sophisticated to the characterful, and there are even one or two trendy neo-hippie places, such as Ambrosia's, in Calle San Lazaro (off Plaza Victoria).

Make a point of seeing the 17th-century **Iglesia Santa María de la Encarnación**, Marbella's main church, from where a signpost leads the way to the **Museo del Grabado** (Monday 11am–2pm, Tuesday to Friday 11am–2pm and 5.30–8.15pm; Sunday 11.30am–2.15pm; closed Saturday), devoted to contemporary art. Look into the tiny **Capilla de San Juan de Dios** (16th-century) and through the grille to its small ornate altar. To the northeast are remains of the **castle and town walls** (walk through Plaza de los Naranjos and up a flight of steps) first raised by the Arabs in the 9th century. Cross Avenida Nabeul into Calle Sagunto and take in the quaint and pretty pedestrianised *calles* of del Río, San Cristobal, San Ramón and Luna.

*Capilla de San Juan de Dios*

After exploring the old town, walk westward along the north side of Avenida Ramón y Cajal, noting smart shop window displays and the modern sculpture and fountain of *La Bella del Mar.* Cross over to the south side into the tropical **Parque de la Alameda** and walk through its shade, past benches decorated with ceramic tiles, to reach the seafront road of Duque de Ahumada and its promenade facing Playa de Venus (if it appeals, look out for signs to the **Bonsai Museum**, 10am–1.30pm and 4–7.30pm). Go right towards the **Puerto Deportivo** and take a walk around the port if you like.

If you fancy a jaunt in a horse-drawn carriage, approach one of the *cocheros* and agree upon a price for a half-hour ride. It will not be less than 2,000 pesetas. You will be taken the length of the seaside promenade and into a mixed residential and commercial area bordered by Avenida Miguel Cano on the east and Calle Arturo Rubinstein on the west. During your ride you will see that development towards the west has generally been of pleasing design and good quality. To the east, old mixes with new along narrow, tree-lined streets. Make a note of any shops whose windows attract you. When the ride is over, return to your car.

The rest of the day explores the nearby coast and hinterland. Head west on the N340, along the 'Golden Mile', passing the Marbella Club and Puente Romano hotels on the left. Noting signs and turn-offs to other places will help you get your bearings for future reference. Puerto Banús comes up on the left with Nueva

*Arab wall and castle tower*

Andalucía on the right. Very soon after San Pedro de Alcántara you cross the Río Guadalmina and take a right turn to Benahavís. The Atalaya Golf and Country Club (tel: 288 2812) is on the left. Proceed through rural landscapes into a narrowing valley until **Benahavís** appears some 8km (5 miles) from the turn-off. Park at the entrance to the village and walk along its main street, Avenida de Andalucía. More than half this village's 2,000 inhabitants are foreign and they have changed Benahavís to suit their tastes. It is pristine and quaint, self-consciously so. Shops and eateries serve the needs of foreign residents and visitors from the coast.

At the end of Avenida de Andalucía is the gallery of Maffini and Carmen, where they exhibit his sculpture and her tapestries. **La Aldea**, a stylish village within a village, was the brainchild of sculptor David Marshall. His gallery here displays some of his stunning metalwork, including practical items such as candlesticks, fireguards, etc. There are *antigues* and home décor shops in the small Plaza Camilo José Cela, named after the Nobel prizewinner for literature who opened La Aldea. Look at the menus displayed outside the village's plethora of eating places and choose one for lunch. (If you have not already made a booking for dinner at La Fonda, then you should find a telephone now.)

*'La Bella del Mar'*

After lunch, drive back to the N340 and follow signs to **San Pedro de Alcántara**. Its beach area used to be delightfully undeveloped, a favourite place for picnics with local families and for horse rides along the sand. Bulldozers have moved in and all is changing. There are plans to build a *puerto deportivo* here. At the roundabout turn into the town. Take care: traffic whizzes past from both directions and you need to be patient. The town really does not have much to detain you except when it is celebrating a *fiesta*. Its inhabitants and foreign residents eagerly proclaim its virtues and many want its independence from Marbella. A drive through the town may be enough. If you want to explore, park where you can, preferably along the village's main drag, Avenida Marqués del Duero, and take a walk along the avenue and in the streets to the right (east). Some of the better shopping is in the small mall of La Galería, *calles* Córdoba, Lope de Mena and adjoining streets. End up in the Plaza de la Iglesia and, if you need it after the walk, take some refreshment at a café alongside the church.

Back in your car, return to the N340 and proceed towards Marbella. The turn-off right into **Puerto Banús** is 3km (1¼ miles) on. Go left before the port's control barrier to find the car park. Spain's first *pueblo*-port, which has been the model for others, was built in the early 1970s. It is a little less fashionable now and showing signs of wear but it is still one of the Costa del Sol's top sight-seeing attractions. Wander at leisure to see the rich collection of luxury boats and head into the back streets to find a string of fashion boutiques. Choose from one of many bars to have a drink and people-watch. The popular **Sinatra Bar** at the far end of the front is a good spot, as is the **Saldaba** pub next door. Take a walk through the adjoining Benabola luxury residential development on the west side and go into the Gray d'Albion mall. Now head back to your hotel to rest, shower and change for the evening.

*Ana María's*

At around 9pm, go back to Plaza de los Naranjos for a pre-dinner drink and people-watching. Much of the varied fauna Marbella attracts will be on display – and it will be on *paseo* under the pinkish light of streetlamps. Join the parade as you make your way to **Restaurante La Fonda** (Plaza de Santo Cristo 9; closed Sunday except during August). I rate this as the top place to dine in Marbella town. Its sister restaurant, Horcher, has long been one of the best in Madrid, and here Ramón Ballesteros maintains the same standards.

In the warm months, try for a table in the delightful interior patio. Waiters are attentive without overdoing it. The cuisine is an imaginative selection of Spanish and international dishes. Across the *plaza* is **Ana María's**. If it is open – and you should check with your waiter – the flamenco show gets into full swing after midnight. Ana María's deep song still gives me a lump in my throat, but there are evenings when the show can degenerate into a tawdry sing-along. When this happens, it is time to leave. The entrance fee includes one drink.

## Málaga

**Sightseeing and shopping in the provincial capital, taking in the splendid cathedral; spend some time on the beach and enjoy a scenic drive to the village of Mijas. In the evening light you can take a look at Cabo Pino, a pretty marina development, and have dinner at one of my favourite restaurants.**

Call La Hacienda (tel: 283 1267/1116) before setting out, and reserve a table for dinner at 10pm. You can drive from Marbella to Málaga in 1¼ hours. Try to get to the city before 10.30am.

Approaching the outskirts along the N340, follow signs to Málaga-Centro Ciudad which will lead you into Avenida Andalucía. When you see a line of modern commercial buildings, keep your eyes open for the large grey block of **El Corte Inglés** department store ahead on the left. Bear right and around the traffic island to pass in front of the building and take the first right turning to enter its underground car park.

Walk back to Avenida Andalucía and turn left along it to cross the bridge over the Río Guadalmedina which is due for a clean-up and prettifying. Keep on the left of the Alameda Principal and left into Calle Torregorda. Ahead is the **Puerta de Atarazanas**, an

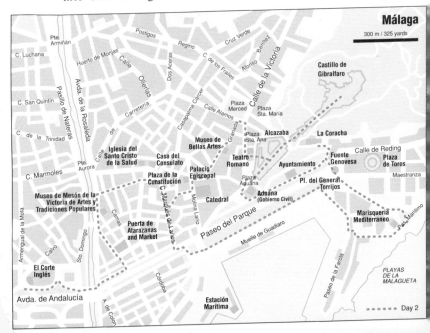

*The cathedral*

11th-century Moorish entrance to what is now Málaga's big, bustling and colourful food market. Walk through to the other end and go straight ahead until you reach the river. On your right is the **Museo de Mesón de la Victoria de Artes y Tradiciones Populares** (10am–1.30pm, 4–7pm winter, 5–8pm summer, closed Saturday afternoon, Sunday and bank holidays), in Paseo de Santa Isabel. The building, completed in 1632, was an inn run by the Franciscans and it is little changed. The museum of arts and popular traditions, created in 1975, occupies its three floors around a central patio. It comprises a fascinating collection from the city's past housed in a charming building.

Turn right when leaving, go first right into Calle Cisneros and continue into Plaza de la Constitución, where there is a stamp and coin market on Sunday. Notable on the north side is the **Casa del Consulado** with a portal of grey marble in baroque style. Left of it, the **Iglesia del Santo Cristo de la Salud**, inaugurated in 1630, shows typical Spanish Mannerist elements. Leave the *plaza* on the right into the Calle Marqués de Larios, the city's main shopping street, which was opened in 1886. Its construction was financed largely by the Larios family whose name is well known for gin and other drinks.

*The Palacio Episcopal*

Turn left into *calles* Strachan and Salinas and you come out in front of the **Catedral** (admission charge; entrance round the side), with the elaborate façade of the **Palacio Episcopal** on your left. The cathedral was begun, in the Gothic style, in 1528 on the site of a mosque. Several style changes followed and today's building is how the project ended up in 1782. The cathedral is popularly known as *La Manquita*, the cripple, because its other tower was never completed. The story goes that funds needed for its completion were diverted to support the American War of Independence. Inside, the most exceptional feature is the *coro* (choir), completed in 1662 by the great Granadan

*The Teatro Romano*

sculptor Pedro de Mena. The 40 tableaux in mahogany, cedar and red ebony are marvellously detailed. Other highlights include the Gothic Chapel of Saint Barbara, to the right of the central chapel of the apse. You can also pop into the archbishop's palace, mainly 18th-century, to see its handsome patio and imperial staircase to the principal floor which houses the **Museo Episcopal** of religious art and objects, which also stages temporary art exhibitions.

Go along the left side of the cathedral, noting the elaborate carving on the portal and, on your left, that of the **Iglesia del Sagrario**, the surviving section of a Gothic church built in 1488. Turn left into Calle San Agustín to reach the **Museo de Bellas Artes** (Tuesday to Friday 10am–1pm and 5–8pm, Saturday, Sunday and holidays 10am–1pm, closed Monday) which is housed in the palace of the Condes of Buenavista, built between 1530–40. The austere exterior and watchtower give the building an unusual martial appearance. Inside, it is graced by a beautiful patio. Twenty rooms exhibit paintings, sculpture, drawings, engravings, ceramics, silverware and furniture dating from the 15th to the 20th century. On the ground floor are works by leading Spanish artists of the 16th and 17th centuries: Morales, Ribera, Murillo, Zurbarán, Alonso Cano and Pedro de Mena. Painters from the Málaga School of the 19th century are well represented. Don't miss the sketches done by Málaga-born Pablo Picasso between the ages of 10 and 14, and paintings by his teacher, Muñoz Degrain.

Exit right and continue turning right into *calles* Granada, Santiago and Alcazabilla. Walking down Alcazabilla, you pass the Casa de Cultura (due for demolition in order to recover more of the Roman theatre in a major redevelopment of this area). Cross over for a look at the **Teatro Romano**, built during the reign of Augustus, and then go into the **Alcazaba**. In the 8th century the Moors began building a fortress on the remains of one left by the Romans. It is connected by a rampart to the **Castillo de Gibralfaro**, a Moorish construction on Phoenician foundations, at the top of the hill. What you see of the Alcazaba today is for the most part a construction ordered by a king of the *taifa* of

*The Fuente Genovesa*

Granada in 1057, which was subject to major renovation in 1933. It gives you an introduction to typical features of Moorish architecture. Double walls with defensive towers surround gardens, patios and reconstructed palaces. The latter now house the small collection of the **Museo Arqueológico** (winter 10am–1pm and 4–7pm; summer 10am–1pm and 5–8pm). Most notable are its Moorish stucco work and ceramics. Note also that a few of the Moorish horseshoe arches are supported on Roman columns and capitals.

Go left when leaving the Alcazaba. The solid square building on your right is the old **Aduana**, completed for the port authorities in 1829 and now housing the central government's delegation in Málaga province. When you reach the tree-lined Paseo del Parque, continue left past the neo-baroque **Ayuntamiento** (City Hall), completed in 1919. Decorative features allude to the city's economic activities of the time. Tourism did not feature then and does not much now. You come to Plaza del General Torrijos and the **Fuente Genovesa**, a Renaissance fountain in marble with aquatic themes in its decoration. **La Coracha**, the row of old houses on the side of Gibralfaro hill, will become

*Alcazaba and Gibralfaro in evening light*

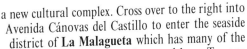

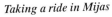
*Taking a ride in Mijas*

a new cultural complex. Cross over to the right into Avenida Cánovas del Castillo to enter the seaside district of **La Malagueta** which has many of the city's best eating places and bars. Try one of the many seafood houses in the area and order *fritura malagueña*, a delicious mixed fish fry which is a local speciality.

Before 4.30pm you should be on your way again. Go west towards the harbour and then along the attractive **Paseo de la Farola**. You pass the statue of *El Cenachero*, dedicated to the Malagueño poet Salvador Rueda. Turn into the **Paseo del Parque** to walk through its elegant gardens which boast 2,000 examples of flowers and trees. Many are identified on painted ceramic tiles. Cross to the right at the Hotel Málaga Palacio, bear left towards a statue of the **Marqués de Larios** and go right up the thoroughfare named after him. If you are in the mood for shopping, now is your chance.

Leave town the way you came in, on the Avenida de Andalucía following signposts to Torremolinos-Airport-Cádiz. After you pass the Aquapark at Torremolinos, go right onto the road signposted for Benalmádena Pueblo. Urbanisation has swallowed up the small *pueblos* of Arroya de la Miel and Benalmádena. After passing what remains of the last village, you have a twisting road of 8km (5 miles) to Mijas from which vantage there are extensive views of the coast. Stop at the Venta Higueron to enjoy them. Ironically, the nearby Urbanización Buena Vista (Good View) looks over a huge rubbish dump. Now go right onto the main road into **Mijas** and, if you can find space, park in the second (upper) car park. The tour coaches will probably have left by now and the *burro* taxis will be on their way home for rest before another day of taking day-trippers around the village's cobbled streets.

*Marqués de Lario*

Foreigners outnumber Spanish residents in the large municipality of Mijas and it is the archetypal tourist *pueblo*. At this time of the day, it should be quite peaceful and, wandering its back streets, you get an idea of how it might have been before the opening of so many tourist eateries and souvenir shops. Walk through the attractive Plaza de la Constitución and past the small square bullring to the main parish church, with some *mudéjar* features. From the gardens beyond, you can look over Mijas Campo, crowded with urbanisation and golf courses. Fuengirola, once a tiny fishing village which until 1841 belonged to Mijas, is just along the coast.

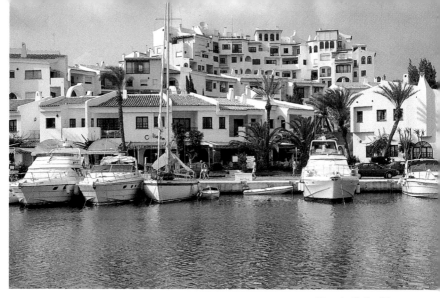

*Puerto Cabo Pino*

Back at the upper car park is the oddest museum you are likely to find. The **Museo Carramota de Max** (closes 7pm) contains a varied collection of the tiniest things imaginable. On the other side of the car park a cave serves as the shrine of the village's patroness, La Virgen de la Peña. Apparently the Virgin Mary appeared to a girl whose family lived in this cave. Votive offerings are pinned to a wall and pilgrims place flowers in front of the tiny altar. In September a festival of the Virgin takes place, with flamenco contests, singing and partying.

Head back for the N340 coastal highway, passing by the luxury villas and hotels you spied from above. Follow signs to Marbella-Cádiz, bypassing Fuengirola. If you have time, bear off right and around to **Puerto Cabo Pino**. This is the newest of Marbella's *pueblo* marinas and, I think, its prettiest. Take a stroll around and have a drink at one of the quayside bars. La Hacienda restaurant is not far away from here in Urbanización Hacienda de Las Chapas (turn off inland from the N340 between km193 and km194). You have to decide now if you want to drive back to wherever you are staying to freshen up or if you are feeling comfortable and are already dressed – casually but smart – for dinner.

**La Hacienda** (closed Monday and Tuesday and from mid-November to December) is the creation of owner-chef Paul Schiff, who was born in Luxembourg and trained and worked at top restaurants in Belgium for 25 years. Schiff came to Marbella in 1969 and his restaurant was voted a member of Relais & Chateaux in 1979. He has won the *Premio Nacional de Gastronomía*, Spain's highest gastronomic award. La Hacienda is now run by Teresa Schiff and her daughter. One is spoiled for choice from the tempting selection described on the seasonal menu. Ask for advice and be inclined to choose the special dishes of the day. The Gastronomic Menu (minimum two persons) consisting of seven courses eases the problem of choice and is very good value.

## Ronda

A scenic drive inland to Ronda, one of Spain's most spectacularly sited towns. If you want to stay the night and take in some horse riding in the hills on the following morning (details from Ronda's tourist office), or head on to Option 10 (page 64), Ronda has plenty of hotels and pensións, including the luxurious **Parador** (tel: 287 7500), perched above the Tajo. For those returning to Marbella, dinner is suggested in **La Meridiana** (advisable to book; tel: 277 6190), one of Marbella's finest restaurants.

Allowing for a few stops to enjoy views and take pictures, you can comfortably drive to Ronda from Marbella within 1½ hours. Try to get there by 10.30am, remembering that the light for picture-taking on the way is better before the heat haze sets in. At the eastern end of San Pedro de Alcántara, turn off the N340 onto the C339. Eight kilometres (5 miles) from the turn-off, a valley on the left has been turned into **Los Arqueros Golf** courses (tel: 281 5873), designed by Severiano Ballestoros. Clinging to a hillside on the right are the attractively coloured buildings of La Heredia, a modern *pueblo*-style residential complex. You then come to the luxury residential area of **El Madroñal** and **El Coto**, a 'hunting lodge'-style restaurant specialising in meat and game. The road is in good condition, wide but twisting, and an average speed of 50kph (30mph)

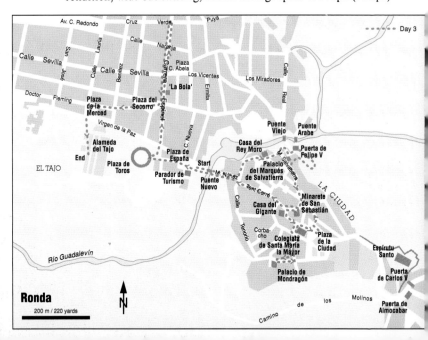

Ronda

200 m / 220 yards

*La Heredia residential complex*

is about the limit. Bashed crash barriers may indicate that some drivers have exceeded it. In early summer, vividly yellow gorse covers the lower slopes. On the left are grand views across the valley of the Río Guadalmina and undulating hills towards the coast and Gibraltar and, perhaps, Africa. While driving this road I have many times seen eagles and vultures soaring above the area where the mountainside is at its starkest in the **Reserva Nacional de la Serranía de Ronda**, a game reserve of 23,000ha (56,834 acres). After about 35km (21¾ miles) you are on the high plateau of the Serranía, the road is less twisting and your average speed can rise to 80kph (50mph). Isolated hamlets lie in the basins of the *ríos* Genal and Guadiaro on the left where land developers have set their sights on creating 'ecological tourism', whatever that may mean. Ronda is soon in sight.

The town sits atop a rocky outcrop in a basin surrounded by the mountains of the Serranía de Ronda. It is 740m (2,428ft) above sea level, the highest of the mountains being some 2,000m (6,562ft). Ronda's municipal territory of 477km² (185 square miles) is one of the largest in Andalusia, yet the town and its 19 rural villages have only 30,000 inhabitants. Livestock and farming have traditionally been the main activities.

The Town Hall has not opted for strengthening the traditional economy. It is collaborating with the developers of 'rural' or 'ecological tourism' and is accused of selling off the birthright of *Rondeños* and classifying land according to the requirements of developers and the investment deals

33

negotiated. Hard-pressed small farmers and absentee owners of big estates have been eagerly selling their land at prices that appear to them to be high but which represent bargains for the developers.

Stop before entering the town (not at the sign 'Peurtas Antiguas' leading along a farm track) to look at the two gateways in the remaining walls: **Puerta de Almocabar**, on the right, was built in the 13th century and gave access to the Moors' *alcazaba* and town; **Puerta de Carlos V** is a typical Renaissance gateway of the 16th century. Remnants of the walls run round to the right. Drive into the town and through the old part, to which you will return on foot. Cross the Puente Nuevo into the newer part of town, *El Mercadillo*, and try to find parking. The best bet is to go through the **Plaza de España** into Calle Virgen de la Paz and take the first left to a public car park. If that is full, continue along Calle Virgen de la Paz to find a space in Plaza de la Merced. If you have no luck

*Puerta de Felipe V*

there, I must leave you to your own devices. Ronda can get very congested at the height of the tourist season. Walk back to Plaza de España and pop into the tourist office to collect any useful literature you require and to ask about any special events.

Ahead is the **Puente Nuevo** (New Bridge) spanning the 'Tajo' (Gorge) across the Río Guadalevín and overlooked by a new parador occupying the site of the old Town Hall. The bridge was built between 1751–93 and is 98m (321ft) at its highest. The architect of what has become the town's symbol met his death for the sake of his hat: as he was being lowered in a basket to inspect his creation, the wind caught his hat and reaching out for it he tipped out into the gorge. The *Tajo* is an impressive sight; it has a compelling fascination for people intent on suicide; also, picadors' horses gored and killed by bulls used to be pushed into the gorge.

Across the bridge, you are again in the old part of town, *La Ciudad*. Turn left into Calle Santo Domingo. On the left, **La Casa del Rey Moro** was not the house of a Moorish king, as the name suggests. It was built in the 1700s as the town house of a wealthy family. Try to see its attractive garden. Behind it the **Mina de Ronda** stairway leads down to the river. If under seige, the Moors used Christian slaves as a water-supply bucket brigade ranged up the stairs. Next to note is the elaborate façade, sculptured balcony and wrought-iron work of the privately-owned **Palacio del Marqués de Salvatierra** which dates from the 18th century.

*View from the southern approach road*

Provided the family isn't in residence, illuminating guided tours of the *palacio* are conducted on the hour from 11am–2pm and from 4–6pm (it's worth checking to see if someone will take you round even if you arrive off the hour). The wrought-iron here is typical of the work of Ronda's renowned forges, and you will see much more of it around the town in *rejas* (window bars), grilles to doorways and on balconies. Continue on left through the **Puerta de Felipe V**, a mini triumphal arch built in 1742 and commemorating Spain's first Bourbon king. Down the slope is the **Puente Viejo** (Old Bridge), built in 1616. From here you have an impressive upward view of the *Tajo* on the left. To the right is the **Puente Arabe**, definitely Moorish but, perhaps, originally Roman. Further right, the **Baños Arabes** have the typical roof shape of Arab baths. Built in the 13th century, the baths are in a fairly good state of preservation and are open 10am–1pm and 4–7pm except Sunday afternoon and Monday. Go back up to the Puerta de Felipe V and bear left up Calle Marqués de Salvatierra.

As you turn right into Calle Armiñán, the main street, on the left the 14th-century **Minarete de San Sebastián** reflects the 'nazarene' architectural features of Granada's Nasrid dynasty which gave us the magnificent Alhambra palace. Next along, off to the left and up José Maria Holdago, is the **Casa del Gigante** (House of the Giant), a Moorish palace of the same period, much changed over the centuries. Go left here to make your way along alleys to **St Maria la Mayor**, dating from the 13th century when it was the principal

*Palacio del Marqués de Salvatierra*

*Plaza de Toros*

mosque. A stone's throw southwest is the **Palacio de Mondragón** (Monday to Friday 10am–6pm, Saturday and Sunday 10am–3pm), first built in 1314 by the Muslim king of Ronda. Little remains of the original except the foundations and underground passages connecting with the *alcazar* ruins. The towers are *mudéjar*, the portal is Renaissance and there are some baroque decorative features.

Wander back to and across the Puente Nuevo towards the **Plaza de Toros** and buy a ticket at the kiosk. The bullring, inaugurated in 1785, is among Spain's oldest and at 66m (216ft) the widest. It was first used for equestrian training and bullfighting from horseback by members of the Real Maestranza de Caballería, a chivalrous order founded by Felipe II in 1573 to toughen up knights going to seed. In the late 1820s, at the age of 72, Pedro Romero ended his career after having killed some 6,000 bulls without once being gored. His grandfather, Francisco, had started the tradition of fighting on foot using the cape and *muleta* (killing sword). Pedro developed the classical style and is considered the father of modern bullfighting. Goya painted him and *corrida* scenes.

Below part of the covered terraces is a museum of bullfighting. If like me you are not an aficionado, you'll be glad to move on. But the town does not let you easily avoid its taurine connections. Cross from the bullring into pedestrianised Carrera Espinel, locally known as *la Bola*. On the left, a photography shop displays photographs of Ernest Hemingway in Ronda. *Ernesto* befriended Antonio Ordóñez, an acclaimed *Rondeño* matador. So did Orson Welles, who is buried on the Ordóñez estate. If you want to see more bullfighting memorabilia go to the Restaurante Pedro Romero, situated opposite the Plaza de Toros.

Along *la Bola* you may be tempted by some of the shops but avoid the tourist trash on display. Craft specialities are bulky — ironwork and saddlery. A lot of the much-lauded Ronda sausage is now made from Dutch pigs as local pork production has declined. Make your way back to **Plaza del Socorro**. The bar of the **Circulo de Artistas** is a good place to observe some of the locals as you sip a *fino*. Afterwards, go left as you leave, to the Plaza de la Merced and into the **Alameda del Tajo**. This park promenade was completed in 1806 with funds raised by fining offenders for indecent behaviour and blasphemy. It was the scene of very indecent behaviour during the Civil War when self-righteous Republicans threw 512 alleged Nationalist sympathisers from its balcony.

Back in your car, return across the Puente Nuevo, through *La Ciudad* and go right as soon as you exit from the town. If you miss this small road, ask someone for the **Camino de los Molinos**. The road twists through olive groves and leads to a spot from which you have the most impressive, most photographed views of the *Tajo* and Puente Nuevo. When you've finished clicking, return the same way. If you are returning to Marbella, take the c339 road.

**La Meridiana**, this evening's restaurant, is in Urbanización Las Lomas de Marbella, reached by taking the road inland from the N340, opposite Puente Romano and next to the mosque. Paolo Guirelli opened his first Marbella restaurant in the Old Town in 1969 and also started Don Leone in Puerto Banús. In 1982 he opened La Meridiana in a new building of dramatic design, exhibiting a creative flair which he has also applied to his cuisine of classical Mediterranean inspiration. Either the *Menu Degustation* or *Menu Gourmand* ease the difficulty of choosing and well reflect the house cuisine. Try the turbot and lobster with sea urchin sauce, or the wild duck. La Meridiana (tel: 277 6190) is open seven nights a week in summer and from Wednesday to Sunday in other seasons.

*The 'Tajo' and Puente Nuevo*

## Antequera

**See monumental architecture in noble Antequera and visit its small gem of a museum. Nearby, enter the lunar landscape of El Torcal; then drive through the verdant green of the Montes de Málaga. It would be a good idea to pack a picnic for today.**

You can drive to Antequera within two hours along the N340 towards Málaga, then taking the N321/331. A new bypass around the western part of Málaga and the gradual completion of the N321/331 dual carriageway has shortened the journey.

Some 40km (25 miles) from Málaga and after a number of tunnels, the N321 reaches the high point of Puerto de las Pedrizas (780m/2,559ft) and the N331 branches off to Antequera (signposted Seville and Córdoba). The road descends and you get your first views of Antequera's rich agricultural plain.

In land area, Antequera is the fifth-largest municipality in Spain, with around 30,000 inhabitants in the town and 12,000 in 11 villages. Agriculture is the economic mainstay, with cereals and olives predominating. Sunflowers, a new and highly productive crop for the area, make a vivid patchwork through the *vega* in early summer. Some 12km (7½ miles) further on, branch left into Antequera.

Before entering the town, watch on the right for a sign mark-

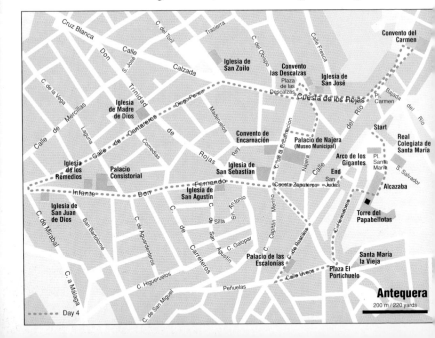

*Burial chamber, Cueva de Menga*

ing the **Conjunto Dolmenico**. There is a car park outside the fenced-off area. Walk in and find the caretaker if the gates to the **Cueva de Menga** and **Cueva de Viera** are locked. The former is the most impressive of these burial chambers, which date from around 2000BC. Little is known about the people who built these chambers or how they managed to haul the stone slabs, quarried in the mountains, to the site and then raise them into position. The total weight of the 31 stones is around 1,600 tons; some slabs weigh 180 tons. The large cave-tombs, in this case measuring 25m (82ft) in depth with a height of 3.5m (11½ft), were then sealed and covered with earth. It is assumed they were the burial places of leaders and their possessions, but looting over the centuries has left no evidence of either.

Back in your car, drive into the town and pick up signs for the Castillo or Alcazaba. Park when you reach the top of the hill. Walk through the **Arco de los Gigantes**, a Mannerist construction from 1585. Looking back, it gives a picture-frame view of the town and its towers. Ahead is the Plateresque façade of the **Real Colegiata de Santa María**, a huge church built between 1514–50, where, according to a plaque on its wall, a group of leading Spanish humanists taught – even though it might be argued that the humanistic emphasis on reason, knowledge and the centrality of man in the scheme of things was incompatible with Christian dogma. The church is a national monument and has recently been restored. From the side of the arch, steps lead up into what remains of the **Alcazaba** which the Moors built in the 14th century on what then remained of a Roman fortress. Now it is mostly a garden overlooked by the bell-tower of **Torre del Papabellotas** (Father Acorns), built in 1582 with funds from the sale of a cork oak plot.

*Torre del Papabellotas*

After the Christians took the town from the Moors in 1410 they started a spree of building churches, convents and monasteries.

*Inglesia de San Sebastián*

Look eastward and you see **La Pena de los Enamorados** (Lovers' Peak) resembling the profile of a reclining figure. The peak has yielded a story of despairing love: Tazgona, daughter of a wealthy Moor from Archidona, was the secret lover of a Christian from Granada, but neither family would permit their marriage. Pursued by her father's men, they climbed the peak and jumped into the abyss — to death and eternal togetherness.

*Real Colegiata de Santa María*

From the Giants' Arch, walk left down Calle Herradores to **Plaza El Portichuelo**, an ornate baroque assembly of the mid-18th century. The street chapel of Santa María la Vieja, one of numerous churches repaired after the ravages of Napoleon's army, is like many seen in Mexico. In the niche of the high altar is the image of the **Virgen de Socorro** which is especially revered by the town. Along Cuesto Alvaro de Oviedo and right into Pastillas, on the right is the **Casa Marques de las Escalonías**, a Mannerist-style palace from the late 16th century which exemplifies the town houses ordered by the artistocracy. Try to see its Arab-style gardens overlooked by three-floored galleries. Turn left into Cuesta del Viento, then go down some steps, and you pass the 17th-century **Iglesia de Santo Domingo**. Dominating the *plaza* of the same name is the **Iglesia de San Sebastián**, 16th-century Renaissance with a striking baroque-*mudéjar* tower. Its interior is filled with painting and sculpture. The *plaza*'s fountain dates from the same century.

Down to the right of the church, and joined to it, is the Carmelite **Convento de la Encarnación**, also 16th-century, with notable *mudéjar* work inside. Opposite the convent is the **Palacio de Nájera**, built in the early 18th century for another rich family. Inside is an attractive patio and the **Museo Municipal** (Tuesday to Friday 10am–1pm, Saturday 10am–1pm, Sunday 11am–1pm, closed Monday). This small and carefully tended museum has a singular prize: the *Efebo*, a life-sized bronze figure of a garlanded boy, was ploughed up in a field in the 1950s. Dated from the 1st century AD and probably a copy of a Greek work, it is among the finest Roman statues found in Iberia.

Go left down Calle Nájera, bearing left to the small and pretty Plaza de las Descalzas ('Barefooted') which is backed by the **Convento de las Descalzas** of the closed order of

*Iglesia de San José*

Carmelites. The church's façade is a good example of Antequera's particular baroque style and, ironically, includes references to pagan mythology in its decoration. Turn up Cuesta de los Rojas, running alongside the convent, and left past the gateway of Postigo de la Estrella to the National Monument of **Convento del Carmen**. It is the remaining part of a Carmelite convent completed in 1633. The rich interior is dominated by three big reredos, the central one of ungilt wood.

Return to Plaza de las Descalzas and go into Calle Calzada, and then right, past the market at Plaza San Francisco, to the National Monument of **Iglesia de San Zoilo Siglio XVII**, which was ordered by the Catholic Monarchs and completed in 1515 in

*Parque Natural El Torcal*

late-Gothic style. If you can, go inside to see *mudéjar* plaster work and the dome over the chancel which were added during remodelling. From Plaza San Francisco, take Calle Diego Ponce past the 18th-century **Iglesia de Madre de Dios**, a good example of Andalusian rococo architecture. When you reach the Alameda de Andalucía, go left into Calle Infante Don Fernando. On the left is the Tourist Office (9.30am–1.30pm and 4–7pm, Sunday 10am–2pm) and then the **Iglesia de los Remedios** (17th-century), dedicated to Antequera's patron saint, Nuestra Señora de los Remedios. The church's convent is now the **Palacio Consistorial** (Town Hall). Its façade is 1950s neo-baroque; the colonnaded cloister dates from the late 17th century; baroque plaster work covers the dome above the grand staircase.

Continue along what is the town's principal shopping street and note the prominent belfry of Iglesia de San Agustín. Go across Plaza San Sebastián and into Cuesta Zapateros and Cuesta San Judas, uphill past whitewashed houses to where your car is parked.

You may want to stop for lunch somewhere along the scenic 16-km (10-mile) drive to **Parque Natural El Torcal de Antequera**. In these 1,200ha (2,965 acres) of protected highland you can wander along marked paths among weird and wonderful limestone formations carved by the elements. There are marked paths: yellow for strolls of one to two hours; red for longer and harder walks of up to three hours. Ivy, wild irises, phlomis, labiates, herbs and holm oaks are among the varied vegetation. At the end of the road from **El Torcal**, go right to **Villanueva de la Concepción**, a sleepy village, and head east along a pot-holed road to **Casabermeja**.

In Casabermeja follow the signpost to Málaga – the camera symbol indicating a road to the right. It is a more scenic route, through the **Parque Natural de Montes de Málaga**. When you rejoin the Málaga/Antequera highway, follow the signs back to Málaga.

## A Day of Indulgence

**After an extravagant lunch, spend the afternoon lazing in the sun. Try some watersports or exercise in a gymnasium. Enjoy a gourmet dinner and then go to a stylish club.**

The plan for today is what very many regular visitors to Marbella follow every day for the whole of their stay. My thinking is that, as an active and inquisitive traveller, you will not want to indulge in 'total relaxation' until you have seen something of the Costa del Sol's great diversity, enjoyed different types of food in a variety of eating places and gained some insight into the local people and their ways.

Top-rated hotels on the seafront have **beach clubs** which are primarily reserved for use by their guests. The public is welcome but 'Members Only' signs mean that entrance can be restricted. It's the relatively high cost of drinks, food and amenities which ensures that the beach clubs attract only the clientele they want. My shortlist includes two east of the town – **Don Carlos** and **Los Monteros** – and two on the western side – **Marbella Club** and **Puente Romano**. The ingredients they offer are much the same, but the mix and

*Los Monteros Beach Club*

prices are different: loungers in the sun or shade by a pool or on the beach; changing and shower rooms with towel service; attentive waiters; barmen who know how to create a good cocktail; a buffet lunch with a wonderful array of fish, seafood, meats, salads, fresh fruits and desserts; a variety of watersports. Opening seasons and times tend to vary, so telephone ahead to ensure that the beach clubs are operating.

*Marbella Club*

**Don Carlos** (N340, km192; tel: 283 1140). The large free-style pool with islands of plants is particularly attractive. The beach rates less highly. Facilities for watersports – windsurfing, waterskiing and sailing – are among the best on the coast and include tuition (tel: 283 1940). At around 4,500 pesetas per head, excluding drinks, the buffet lunch is the cheapest of the four.

**Los Monteros – La Cabane** (N340 km187; tel: 277 1700). Low thatch-roofed buildings surround a large, rather featureless outdoor pool. There is a tropical environment within a glass enclosure which has a heated pool. It adjoins a terrace well screened from sea breezes. The Buffet-Grill is reasonably priced. A masseur is on hand for inducing even more relaxation.

**Marbella Club** (N340 km178; tel: 277 1300). This has the most intimate ambience and a well established look – it is the oldest. Verdant growth surrounds a freshwater pool. Loungers line a beach of white sand backed by trees and there is a wooden jetty for small craft. The fitness centre has a good range of exercise equipment and includes an invigorating jacuzzi; a sauna and masseur are available on request. There is an excellent buffet lunch (5,600 pts), as well as an à la carte menu.

**El Puente Romano** (N340 km177.5; tel: 277 1700). A wide beach of white sand is protected by a groyne and wharf for small craft. The bar and restaurant are in a rustic structure where the buffet is laid out in an old fishing boat. It is an elaborate display of the freshest fish and seafood for preparation to order. Suggestions and explanations are offered by the *maître d'*. Prices displayed on a blackboard are by weight. Windsurfing gear is available for hire. A new beach club is planned on the west side.

**Fresh fish at El Puente Romano**

In contrast to the exclusivity of the beach clubs is the informality of cheap and cheerful **Victor's Beach** (N340 km177) in the Ancón urbanisation. It's one of the last old-style *chirinquitos* (beach cafés) along the shore and has so far resisted demolition under the new *Ley de la Costa* (Coast Law). Victor is an amiable host, the food is simple, prices are low.

My suggestion is that tonight you should dine at the **Marbella Club Restaurant Grill**, preceded by drinks in the attractive lounge bar or on the terrace. You will be in the place which established Marbella's image and is still very much at the heart of the town's social life. Quality meat and fish is grilled to perfection.

*Victor's Beach*

After dinner, move on just down the road to the **Olivia Valère Club** in the Puente Romano complex or head for Puerto Banus and Latin dancing at **Taco Laco** on the seafront. Some clubs in Puerto Banus don't even open their doors until 4am.

When you go to bed you can reflect on the thought that Marbella's Moors may have been defeated in 1485 but Arabs are back in force with the power of their money. Both the Marbella Club and Puente Romano are now Arab-owned; across the road from the latter is Marbella's new mosque and adjoining it the palace of the Saudi Arabian king.

*Live music at Olivia Valère*

## Half-Day Itineraries

### 1. Morning or Afternoon in Istàn

**A morning or afternoon drive to the mountain village of Istán quickly introduces you to the countryside which lies so close to the developed coastal strip. Have lunch at a 'mesón' on your way to or from Istán, or at one of the restaurants or tapas bars in the village.**

Turn off the N340 at km177, just west of Puente Romano and the mosque. The 16-km (10-mile) long road (C427) is narrow, pot-holed and unmarked but presents no problem to cautious drivers. After 2km (1¼ miles, past the Club Sierra and urbanisation, you start to feel you are in the country. Big, established villas are scattered to the left – good buys when land here was very cheap. With the Sierra Blanca rising steeply on the right, the road twists through small folding hills. Avocado and citrus trees make the valley below look very lush.

On the left is the suggested lunch stop, **Mesón El Potro**, closed from January to end-March and on Monday. At Sunday lunch time

*Istán village*

it is very popular. It's cosy inside; on the pleasant terrace the wasps can be over-attentive. Yves may slightly confuse your order but the cooking is good. The choice is limited and meats are the speciality; chicken the cheapest at around 1,000 pesetas; *solomillo* at 1,600. Delicious home-baked bread is served warm with parsley and garlic butter.

Back on the road, you soon see the wall of the **Embalse de la Concepción**, supplier of water to the coast. Dry scrubland of juniper, gorse and wild herbs has pockets of cork oak and olives. Some of the slopes are terraced. Soon you are in the municipal area of **Istán**. Pine, fig, citrus and carob trees join the vegetation mix, added to in spring by many wild flowers. The mountain rises on the right, *cortijos* dot the view to the left. Just below Istán, you pass the Ermita de San Miguel in the rockface, to which villagers make a *romería* at the end of September during their annual fair. Don't be put off by the messy buildings on the approach to the village. Park on entering the village itself.

There is nothing of special note to see in Istàn but a walk along its narrow, crooked *calles* does give the impression that this is a very old village and probably not much has changed in domestic building style and street layout since it was founded by the Moors during the 9th century. Water is plentiful and its burbling sound is heard almost everywhere. No wonder the Moors liked the place. If you want to see the village's single 'monument', ask at the town hall for keys to the *Torre Arabe*: the tower features a Moorish arch.

Most of the working people

*Local life in Istán*

in a population of 1,600 have jobs on the coast. Fewer now till the small plots, tend the orange and lemon trees in the valley or herd the sheep and goats which sustained most families until quite recently. A few run bars with retired men as weekday regulars and a clientele of day-trippers over weekends. Stop in one for some refreshment and take in the local life.

Take the same road back into Marbella. You have absolutely no option, as beyond the village lies the Serranía de Ronda hunting reserve.

## 2. Lunch at the Refugio de Juanar

**A morning drive to the village of Ojén and on for lunch at a 'refugio' in a part of the Serranía de Ronda hunting reserve – plus an eagle's view over Marbella.**

Turn off the N340 onto the C337 on the eastern edge of Marbella town. It's 19km (11¾ miles) to the Refugio de Juanar. After the outskirts of Marbella the road twists up between fir and eucalyptus trees. Terraces of citrus trees are stepped down to a *barranco* (ravine) on the right. After the Venta Barranco there's a view of **Ojén** to which the road snakes down. The village faces southeast above the green valley of the Río Real where fertile ground for cultivation is not wasted. Park along the main road and walk into the village. Although many of its 2,000 inhabitants now commute to work in Marbella and quite a lot of the village has been modernised, in its cobbled *calles* and *plazas* there is still the feel of a

*View from the mirador near Refugio de Juanar*

*Country-style dining at the Refugio*

typical *pueblo* – old women in black contrasting sharply with whitewashed walls, wrinkled men yawn in the shade, children run in and out through the curtains of tiny doorways.

After the village the scenery gets more dramatic as the road twists up to the Puerto de Ojén pass (580m/1,903ft). A turn-off left (signposted Juanar) and the road goes 5.5km (3½ miles) into the nature reserve's stark landscape to an oasis of trees surrounding the **Refugio de Juanar** (tel: 288 1000) where peacocks often proudly display their plumage in welcome. The Refugio was built by the state-run Parador organisation on the foundations of a hunting lodge of the Larios family (see Day 2). Its staff formed a co-operative to take it over and with the help of provincial authorities they have made it a very comfortable and friendly hostelry. Game is a speciality of the kitchen, and a log fire blazes in the bar in winter (some of the bedrooms also have fireplaces). The menu of the day is excellent value at 2,000 pesetas and the servings could feed a giant. If you prefer, bar snacks are available. Instead of driving, you can walk off the lunch along the road of 2.5km (1½ miles) through a sea of olive trees to the **mirador**. From this vantage point more than 1,000m (3,281ft) above sea level there is a marvellous view over green valleys and hills to Marbella and, sometimes, across to Africa.

Back at the refugio, if you are feeling energetic and have brought walking shoes, you could follow part of the forested trails into the Sierra Blanca, to Istán or Ojén.

## 3. Morning in Estepona

**Morning excursion to Estepona; a drive into the wooded Sierra Bermeja; Puerto de Estepona; lunch in the country or quayside.**

West on the N340 it's a quick 25km (15½ miles) to **Estepona**. Park if you can along the Avenida de España, running alongside the beach. The tourist office (Monday to Friday 9am–3pm, Saturday 10am–1pm) is at the eastern end of the adjoining Paseo Marítimo. Enquire here about any special events, exhibitions and the like. Cross over into Calle Santa Ana and wander at will around the old town.

There is nothing of particular note but the quarter is pretty and im-

*In the old town*

*Puerto de Estepona*

maculately kept – whitewashed buildings beneath tiled roofs have flower-filled balconies and solid *rejas* (grilles) across their windows. Street names are painted on ceramic tiles. In the warm months there are café tables in the attractive **Plaza de las Flores**, once a venue for bullfights. In the Casa de Cultura at its eastern end there may be an exhibition of interest. In Calle Castillo are remnants of the walls of a castle first built by Moors and rebuilt after the Christians took the town in 1456. Behind the ruins is the bustling weekday food market. The town's clock tower symbol, **Torre del Reloj**, remains from a 15th-century church. The nearby replacement parish church of Los Remedios was built in the 18th century. As you wander the back streets keep an eye open for art and craft shops.

Estepona has seen an explosion of residential development in recent years, although this has since slowed. What makes the municipality different from others along the coast is that agriculture is still very important in the lives of many of its 25,000 residents and its development and diversification are being actively supported by local authorities. You see evidence of this on your drive into the Sierra Bermeja. Growing lemons has been a principal activity; now more profitable tropical fruits are being harvested. A monument on the Paseo Marítimo honours local farmers and fishermen, Estepona also still has a sizeable fishing fleet.

Back in your car take Calle La Terraza which dissects the old town and is signposted 'Jubrique'. The road is in good shape and rises through agricultural lands

*Estepona old town*

to the starker slopes of the Sierra Bermeja and Peñas Blancas pass. About 15km (9¼ miles) from the town turn off to **Los Reales** to enter a wooded area where streams burble and roe deer, genets and foxes hide. Marked paths lead deeper into the woods and to examples of the pinsapo fir – everybody's idea of what a Christmas tree should look like – which is indigenous to the area and only grows above 1,000m (3,281ft). The high point, **Alto Los Reales** (1,450m/ 4,757ft), looks out over the coast some 8km (5 miles) away, to Gibraltar, Africa and, on a clear day, even to Seville.

Return the same way. About 2km (1¼ miles) before the town is the **Venta Los Reales** where you can stop for a hearty lunch of unfussy country dishes with good quality ingredients. Rabbit, done in various ways, is a speciality. Go through the town and west to **Puerto de Estepona** where the fishing fleet ties up next to small pleasure craft and ocean-going vessels. The port does not have the glamour of Puerto Banús but is no less attractive for that. On Sunday morning it is the scene of one of the Costa del Sol's liveliest *mercadillos* with stalls selling arts and crafts, secondhand bric-a-brac, clothes and housewares. If you did not have lunch at the *venta*, choose from one of the many places lining the quays. Then, it's back to Marbella or you may like to continue with Itinerary 4.

## 4. Morning or Afternoon in Casares

**A morning or afternoon drive to Casares, one of Spain's most photographed 'pueblos'; a dip into sulphurous waters where local legend has it Julius Caesar bathed; lunch or dinner at a laidback oasis among the vineyards; a look at Puerto Duquesa.**

Go west along the N340 beyond Estepona, past Costa Natura (tel: 280 1500), the first residential complex in Spain's for nudists, and just after the km147 mark turn right to Casares. There are no markings on the narrow road of 14km (8¾ miles) but it is usually in fair condition. As along other minor roads inland from the coast you are quickly transported into a scene very different from the coast's concrete ribbon. Eucalyptus trees line both sides of the road; then you have a view of the Sierra Bermeja's

*Puerto Duquesa in Manilva*

heights with undulating hills below on which *cortijos* are scattered. Eight kilometres (5 miles) along, the road narrows and rises among cork oaks. On a bend is the rustic Venta Victoria. A little further on are good views across to the coast and after 3km (1¼ miles) an **art gallery** (Monday, Wednesday and Friday 10am–2pm).

*Casares, view from the north*

Around a corner is **Casares**, a confection of white cubes on a mountain spur topped by the brown outline of an *alcazar*. There are several roadside bars-cum-restaurants on the road overlooking the town, all with pleasant terraces. Further on, turn left and do the locals a favour by parking at the entrance to their *pueblo*. In the typical Plaza de España is a statue of Blas Infante, born in Casares in 1885, who led the Andalusian Nationalist movement and was murdered by Franco's supporters. Uphill along narrow *calles* is what remains of the **Moorish castle**, not much to see in itself but an excellent vantage point. A morbid thought: hundreds of *moriscos* (descendants of the Moors) who raised a revolt in the early 16th century were rounded up and hurled to their deaths from here.

Back on the road which skirts the town, follow signposts to Manilva and you start getting a different view of Casares. Soon you see the vineyards of Manilva, known for its production of good table grapes and a lively *vino de terreno*. Near a quarry on the town's edge, take a track on the left (it may be signposted **Baños Romanos**) to the river and go left along it for about 1.5km (1 mile). From the outside, the baths don't look like much; inside are Roman arches and the water is invitingly clear. Julius Caesar was here a few decades BC and locals like to believe the waters cleared a skin problem he had. Go back and follow signs to the **Roman Oasis** (lunchtime only April and May; lunch and dinner June to September). Relax with a drink in a hammock and choose from barbecues and dishes with an English touch.

**Manilva** is unremarkable but you may want to stop at a backstreet *bodega* to sample a glass of the local *vino*. Continue to the N340 and go right until the turn-off for **Puerto Duquesa**, another of the Costa del Sol's *pueblo* ports with shops, bars and restaurants and, of course, an array of luxury yachts and cruisers.

# Full-Day Itineraries

**Gaucín for lunch at an old 'fonda'; into Cádiz province; the hideaway of Castellar de la Frontera; Sotogrande's modern marina.**

Start off after 11am and follow *Pick & Mix* Itinerary 4 to Casares. From the road which skirts the village, go right on the MA539, signposted Gaucín. For the next 16km (10 miles) you should exercise caution along the narrow road. Falcons fly above the hushed and starkly beautiful land as the road meanders down to the Río Genal and up the other side to where **Gaucín** sits high above the valley.

*Typical 'cortijo' in Gaucín*

Park where you can in the village. Up until 1.30pm the caretaker should be around to let you into what remains of the 13th-century Moorish **Castillo de Agilla**. In 1848 the powder magazine blew up and destroyed much of the place. Gúzman el Bueno, defender of Tarifa, died here during a battle against the Moors in 1309 (*see Itinerary 11*). The church is sanctuary to a much-revered image of the Child Jesus.

The **Fonda Nacional** (Calle Juan de Dios 8) has been open since the 1860s and it retains its old-world feel. Once called the Hotel Inglés, it was much used by the members of Gibraltar's garrison as an overnight stop on the way to and from Ronda. You can see what they thought of it by looking through a photocopy of the old register book. The dining-room serves inexpensive local fare.

*View of Gaucín village and castle*

*Puerto de Sotogrande*

Leave Gaucín on the C341 signposted Algeciras and 2km (1¼ miles) on look back for a good view of the village. The road drops through gorse and grass-covered hills past picturesque *cortijos* near which horses and cattle are sheltered. After 13km (8 miles) it enters Cádiz province and crosses the Río Guadiaro. This is bull-raising country: 3km (1¾ miles) after the hamlet of San Pablo you see a bull ranch on the left. The white profile of **Jimena de la Frontera** is outlined against a hill, not surprisingly topped by a ruined castle. Quite a few foreigners in search of the real Spain have settled around the village, in the process affecting the authenticity of what they sought.

Continue south on what's now the C3331 past meadows where cattle graze and through avenues of eucalyptus trees until, 14km (8¾ miles) from Jimena, there's a tiny road to the right leading to **Castellar de la Frontera**. Villagers readily abandoned this isolated place when Nuevo Castellar was built for them on the main road. You'll understand why and also why alternative life-stylers wanting to get away from it all moved in with their odd assortment of transport and took over some of the houses. The remains of a castle once crucial on the *frontera* (frontier) between Christians and Arabs broods over the newcomers' hideaway and the waters of the Embalse de Guadarranque reservoir. A very narrow but extremely scenic road weaves southward to the C3331.

Go left and into Nuevo Castellar to pick up a back road to Sotogrande. At the N340 coastal highway, go left (east) and then soon right at the sign to **Puerto de Sotogrande**. It's a recently completed marina in 'modern Mediterranean' style, different from the more usual *pueblos*. Here you may want to have a drink and watch the sun, unlike the Union Jack, go down over Gibraltar. It is an easy run of some 50km (31 miles) back to Marbella.

## 6. Ardales, Lakes, El Chorro

**Impressive scenery: white towns and villages; Carratraca's spa; to the lake district for lunch; spectacular El Chorro gorge. You may want to combine this itinerary with No 12, in which case Ardales is an attractive place to spend the night. There is a small pensión on the road below the village or the spotless and homely Pensión Bobastro on the main street.**

Start at around 10am and follow *Pick & Mix* Itinerary 2 to Ojén. Between Ojén and Monda the road passes through a stark landscape and a small gorge. Nineteen kilometres (11¾ miles) from Marbella, **Monda** is a sleepy place. Retired or jobless men watch

*Ardales*

traffic passing as they sit in the Central Café. The new road bypassing the town will deny them this entertainment. Anticipating the easier access to the coast, urbanisations are growing around the town and the Moorish fortress is being rebuilt as a hotel.

Ten kilometres (6¼ miles) on is **Coín**, described by one Moorish writer as 'a beautiful place with lots of springs, trees and fruit'. The terracing and irrigation of the productive surrounding area are legacies of the Moors. Much of the 22,000 inhabitants' socialising occurs on the tree-lined *rambla*. Park nearby if you want a quick wander: the maze of narrow streets follows the old Moorish layout; modern buildings are juxtaposed with old ones; two churches, Santa María and San Juan Bautista, are of *mudéjar*-Renaissance style (the former was originally a mosque).

Leave Coín on the MA422 to Cártama (take the Malaga road out of town) and you pass through varied countryside. Across the Río Guadalhorce, turn left on the MA402 and head up the fertile valley where citrus and avocados grow in abundance. Pizarra is a village to pass quickly. Soon the outline of **Alora**'s castle appears above white houses dripping down the hill on either side. Phoenicians, Romans, Vandals, Moors and Christians played a role in its history. Although many new buildings are evidence of the increased prosperity from agriculture of its 10,000 inhabitants, the town retains some pretty old parts. It took the whole 17th century to complete its church, which has the distinction of being the second largest in Málaga province.

*The lake district*

From Alora go west to Ardales, for a scenic drive through the rugged Sierra de Alcaparain and Sierra de Aguas. **Carratraca** (right turn off the road) began as a village in the last century on the site of the '*cortijo* of foul smelling waters' and flourished as a spa for the rich and famous. Six hundred litres (158 gallons) per minute of sulphurous waters, especially recommended for respiratory and skin complaints, gush from the ground at around 16°C (61°F). In 1830 Fernando VII had a hostelry built for members of his court. It survives as the delightfully old-world Hostal del Príncipe.

Continue through a landscape of almond and olive trees and soon **Ardales** presents a striking aspect against hills on the left. Above the white houses the ochre outlines of its castle and the *mudéjar* tower of its church stand proud. It was Roman engineers who first built the bridge across the river below. (There are two small *pensíons* if you want to stay the night: a roadside inn just outside town and the comfortable Pensión Bobastro in the centre.)

Bear right at the junction after the town and very soon you are in Málaga's lake district. Three lakes fed by the Guadalhorce and other rivers supply much of the province's water. Continue through pine trees into the **Parque de Ardales**, a recreation park created by ICONA, Spain's environmental agency. **El Mirador**, above a small tunnel, is an unpretentious place for lunch and it has a good view of the reservoir. Further on and across a dam wall is **El Oasis**, smarter and pricier. Note the stone seat from which Alfonso XIII declared the Guadalhorce dam scheme open in 1921.

Back at the T-junction go left and a few kilometres on turn right for a drive of 6km (3¾ miles) to the **Ruinas de Bobastro** at over 600m (1,968ft). Omar Al-Hafsun mobilised a rebel kingdom against Córdoba in the 9th century and Bobastro was his stronghold. Little remains, but it is worth walking to see a *mozarabe* church shaped from the rock.

*El Camino del Rey at El Chorro*

Back in your car, proceed downhill for **El Chorro**. Watch on the left for the wooden catwalk hanging precariously on the cliffside. Stop when you can see the entrance to the deep cleft of **La Garganta** (The Throat). The **El Camino del Rey** (Path of the King) catwalk was used by Alfonso XIII when he opened the dam scheme in 1921. Continue towards Alora. On the way back to Marbella via Estación de Cártama, either go via Coín or turn left to Churriana and the N340. You may want to link up with *Pick & Mix Itinerary 8*, and take in Torremolinos.

## 7. La Axarquìa, Nerja, Frigiliana

**Set out at around 9am, to go east of Málaga into La Axarquía, a scenic area packed with pretty villages, to visit the resort of Nerja, its spectacular caves and the award-winning, pristine village of Frigiliana.**

Even allowing for traffic congestion in Málaga, it should not take more than 2½ hours to drive from Marbella to Nerja. New bypasses around Málaga will shorten the journey. There is little to detain you in the resorts of Torre del Mar, Algarrobo Costa and Torrox Costa. Their growth from fishing villages is relatively recent and they cater for Spanish and foreign families who want a quieter, cheaper seaside holiday on the Costa del Sol. Fields of sugar cane, first introduced by the Moors, cover much of the flatlands. And so does plastic, under which up to three crops of vegetables and salad produce can be grown each year.

**Nerja** has seen spectacular growth and it has not all been well controlled. Drive into the town following signs to the **Balcón de Europa** and there's a car park nearby. King Alfonso XII declared this promontory to be the balcony of Europe when he visited the town in 1885 during a tour of the south coast to commiserate with the people following an earthquake. Yes, the south coast does lie along a geological fault line. Like Californians, forget that thought and take in the views before having some refreshment at an outdoor café. Waves of variegated English accents pass by. Nerja is very much a British enclave, and has been for many years.

In addition to the usual tourist tat, Nerja has some good shopping, especially along *calles* Cristo and Pintada. Surviving among the commercialism are old houses whose heavy doorways hide plant-filled patios. Along these streets and those connecting them is an international collection of bars and eateries. Attractive beaches lie

*Frigiliana, one of Spain's prettiest villages*

*Cuevas de Nerja*

below the cliffs, small coves nearest the town and long Playa de Burriana to the east with the Parador sited above it.

Four kilometres (2½ miles) east on the N340, just past the aqueduct, are the **Cuevas de Nerja** (9.30am–9pm in summer; 10.30am–2pm and 3.30–6pm in winter). In 1959 young boys in search of bats discovered these caves, which are among the world's most spectacular. Evidence of Cro-Magnon man's habitation of them some 20,000 years ago has been found here by archaeologists. Also on the road to **Maro** is what is left of a Roman aqueduct. Other evidence of the Roman settlement of Detunda

*The balcony of Europe*

*Frigiliana craft shop*

appears in the intensively worked patchwork of terraced plots stepping down to the sea around this delightfully unspoilt hamlet. From its *balcón* you can look along the dramatic coastline of Granada province where mountains drop sharply to the Mediterranean. Return to just west of Nerja and follow the signpost to Frigiliana and the *Ruta del Sol y del Vino*.

**Frigiliana** appears as a white splash against the greyish lower folds of the Sierra Tejeda. Terraces of vegetables, vines and fruit trees lie below. Park at the village entrance near the old sugar factory and walk left up into the oldest part where dazzling white buildings line stepped streets. Ceramic tiles tell the tale of the village's valiant fight against Felipe II's troops during the *morisco* rebellion of 1569. A translation is available from the **Garden Bar** (closed Tuesday) high above the town; stop for lunch here if the weather is good, the barbecue and bistro menu often features succulent roast lamb, served under thatched parasols. Alternatively, near the church is **La Boquetilla** for tasty local fare. **La Cesta** has a good display of genuine craft items and also sells **Frigiliana**'s tasty and strong *vino de terreno* which is typical of the Axarquía's small-scale production. The whitewashed beds you see near local *cortijos* are for sun-drying moscatel grapes for raisins and wines with a high sugar content.

Take the road below the village and follow signs to **Torrox**. Take care along the 14km (8¾ miles) of this road, which curves high above steep drops. Olives and vines, introduced by Greeks whose colony of Mainake was near Vélez-Málaga, contrast with the deep green of avocado and subtropical fruits. At Torrox go northwards towards Cómpeta, 15km (9¼ miles) away through more attractive scenery.

*Aqueduct near Nerja*

Park at the entrance to **Cómpeta** and look in at **La Posada** where two potters sell their work and other local crafts. Village houses and outlying *cortijos* have been modernised by foreigners, most notably Britons and Danes. Cómpeta is famous in the Axarquía for its *vino de terreno*. It flows freely during the *Noche del Vino* on 15 August.

The road zig-zags down past Sayalonga and Algarrobo to rejoin the N340 some 19km (11¾ miles) away. It's time to go west into the setting sun.

**59**

# Evening and Night-time Itineraries

**Puerto de Benalmádena; Torremolinos, the epitome of a mass-tourism resort; dinner followed by flamenco or other entertainment, and an animated gay scene if you want it.**

Leave Marbella before 6pm and go east along the N340 to Benalmádena Costa, turning right into **Puerto de Benalmádena**. This new sport-port and residential development is intended to be the most up-market area of the urban mass, or mess, along this increasingly built-up part of the Costa del Sol.

**Torremolinos** is and looks tired. The local authorities and others involved in its tourism industry say they are going to revive the old girl who over the years has provided so many good times for so many people on low-cost holidays. There is some evidence that they mean what they say. I, for one, hope that, even if they tart up the town, they won't destroy its appeal of being loud, brash and cheap. Snobbish and sensationalist reporters often give Torremolinos a bad press which open-minded visitors may feel it does not deserve.

From the N340 take the road into Torremolinos and quite soon bear right at the sign for **Playa de Carihuela** to take a stroll along the promenade which is lined by fish restaurants. You'll see that Torremolinos has wide and well serviced beaches, one reason for the resort's popularity. Back in your car, go right at the main road and right at the sign to Calle Casablanca. Park where you can. The tourist office at Danza Invisible 516 (in the Nogalera complex) may be open to inform you about anything special going on.

Crossing Casablanca is pedestrianised **Calle San Miguel** – the magnet for shoppers and strollers; in fact, everybody in Torremoli-

*Calle San Miguel*

nos. It and the streets and arcades around are packed with shops and eateries. Prices here are generally much lower than they are in Marbella.

At the seaward end of San Miguel is a 14th-century Moorish *torre* (tower) and winding steeply down from it the **Cuesta del Tajo** goes through what remains of the original fishing village. On the way is the 16th-century **Molino de Rosario**, one survivor of numerous flour mills which were fed by a stream since diverted. From the *torre* and *molinos* the town got its name. At the end of the walkway is Playa Bajondillo. Here and in the area of Playamar to the east a mass of concrete high-rises lines the shore road.

Back in Calle San Miguel take a seat at the **Bar Toro** where you can observe the passing scene and over a drink decide what you want to do for the rest of the evening and night. Here are some choices. You could stay in Torremolinos: have dinner and see a flamenco show or enjoy other entertainment. Off Calle Casablanca is the Pueblo Blanco arcade which has a collection of restaurants from which to choose. For after-dinner entertainment, **Pepe Lopez**, Plaza Gamba Alegre (the other side of San Miguel), is a popular flamenco venue which may be open. Or there should be live music at a bar nearby. If you are here in the summer, some 80 discos will be operating, many of which are to be found concentrated around the Plaza Costa del Sol at the top of Calle Danza Invisible. These are by and large mostly for the young and lively. **The Palladium**, Avenida Palma de Mallorca 36 (a little way west from the plaza), is definitely the most spectacular nightclub in town with no fewer than four dance floors and a pool.

*Bar Toro*

Torremolinos is popular with gay people and quite a few places cater exclusively, or almost so, for a gay clientele. There is a choice of scenes from suave to heavy in the La Nogalera (near the tourist office), Pueblo Blanco and Edificio Jardín complexes.

Instead of staying in Torremolinos, you may want to return to **Puerto de Benalmádena**, which also gets quite animated at night in the warmer seasons, where you can select from a choice of eating places. For entertainment, see what's on at Puerto Rociero with its flamenco ambience or the Cervecería New York, which often has live music and a jolly foreign clientele. Another possibility is is to have a meal and then move on to the Fortuna Night Club at Torrequebrada (see *Pick & Mix* Itinerary 9).

*Fuengirola, fishing boats and high-rise blocks*

## 9. Café Royale and Fortuna Night Club

**A quick look around Fuengirola and on to the Hotel Torreque-brada for dinner, international floor shows and, if you like, some gambling at the casino.**

Fuengirola is one of Spain's less hectic resorts and has most appeal for young families and older people at whom its accommodation, shops, eateries and entertainment are targeted. It's a bit more expensive than Torremolinos but cheaper than Marbella. Its seven kilometres (4¼ miles) of continuous beach is well tended and serviced. Try to reach **Fuengirola** at around 6pm and just before crossing the bridge over its river turn off right to the **Castillo Sohail**. A fortification, built here by the Moors in the 10th century, was destroyed by the Christians when they took the town in 1485. A new castle was built in 1730 to help in the control of illicit trade with Gibraltar. After extensive renovation, it will be opening as a cultural centre. From the castle there are good views of Fuengirola and across the white-bespeckled Campos de Mijas to Mijas *pueblo*.

Drive into Fuengirola and follow signs to the **Puerto**. Here sport and luxury craft are berthed near traditional fishing boats against a backdrop of modern high-rises. On summer nights the Puerto area is the most animated in town. Park along the Paseo Marí-

timo near El Monumento del Pescador, a reminder that Fuengirola was an insignificant fishing village until a few decades ago. Now walk into the fishing port (on the left, you will pass a small nameless cafe-bar which serves excellent seafood

*Fortuna nightclub*

*tapas* and beer to fishermen and yachting types) and climb up onto the mole, a favourite evening walkway offering good views of the bay. Afterwards return to Paseo Marítimo, turn left and then right up *calles* España or Miguel de Cervantes and dip into the pedestrian streets off them. Here in the **Casco Viejo** (Old Quarter) are many of the most interesting shops, bars and restaurants. The newly renovated **Plaza de la Constitución** is overlooked by the parish church and is a pleasant place to stop for a drink while observing the locals and visitors, as is the **Plaza del Ayuntamiento**, in front of the Town Hall.

Back in your car follow signs to Málaga. Eight kilometres (5 miles) from Fuengirola the solid block of the **Hotel Torrequebrada** fills a small promontory. The **Café Royale** (tel: 244 1643), is an elegant semi-circular restaurant whose wide windows give a view of the coast's sweep glittering with lights, often against a pink sky. The menu has international staples as well as some interesting innovations. It is not cheap, but for what it offers in ambience, attentive service and clever cooking, prices are reasonable.

In the building is the south coast's only night-club with large-scale floor shows. The **Fortuna Night Club**'s first presentation at 10.30pm is of colourful Spanish ballet and flamenco; at midnight there are international presentations of a high standard. Prices are very reasonable and include a drink or two. Between shows or afterwards you can adjourn to the fully-fledged **casino** (tel: 244 2545 for reservations), which stays open until 5am (4am in winter). There's an entrance charge, however, and you must present your passport to gain admission.

*International floor show at the Fortuna*

# EXCURSIONS

## 10. Sierra Villages, Fresh Trout and Caves

**Monumental town, Roman ruins, beautiful mountain scenery, prehistoric cave paintings, white villages, good crafts shopping. Stay overnight in Grazalema, a base for hiking in the Sierra de Grazalema, either in the Hostal Grazalema (tel: 56-141162), a mini-parador on the outskirts of the village, or in the excellent and inexpensive Fonda Garcia (tel: 56-132014).**

Follow the Day 3 itinerary to **Ronda**. After seeing the town and having lunch, take the c339 road signposted 'Seville' and a few kilometres on go right at the sign for **Ronda la Vieja**. After a scenic drive the Roman settlement of Acinipo with its reconstructed theatre is signposted. Eight kilometres (5 miles) on is the unusual sight of a town squeezed into a cleft. Many of **Setenil**'s houses have

roofs formed by the overhanging rock which also shades the streets. One can only hope it remains firmly in place. Backtrack a bit and take the road to El Gastor through peaceful countryside. Go left (direction Ronda) when you reach the c339 and after 3km (1¾ miles) turn right onto a minor road leading to **Grazalema**.

This is one of Spain's prettiest *sierra* villages and its wettest. Rain-filled clouds, borne on Atlantic winds, billow up against El Torrejón and other peaks, releasing their load. In some years the rainfall exceeds 3,000 litres (793 gallons). Grazalema is also a favourite base for hiking: pick up information on walks in the area from the tourist office in the centre of the village.

The Hostal Grazalema, one of the suggested overnight stops, is off the village's approach road.

*Hostal Las Truchas*

It is a mini-parador in regional style with comfortable rooms and a pool. Alternatively try Fonda Garcia in the village. Both have good restaurants. Other places to eat include El Tajo Bar Restaurant next to the municipal swimming pool which offers wonderful views; more simply, Zulema bar offers a wide selection of tasty *raciones*.

Wool weaving was once an important local industry and the village gained fame for the quality of its cloth and *mantas* (blankets). In the last decade initiatives for the revival of this skill have been taken. The **Fabrica de Mantas y Museo** (Monday to Thursday, 10am–2pm and 3–6.30pm) to the right just on entering the village, is a museum-piece factory in operation.

Opposite the camping site on the road to El Bosque is the factory producing another product which has brought the village fame beyond its enclosing *sierras*. Grazalema's *queso de cabra* is a hard goat's milk cheese; one or more of the small yellow rounds makes a tasty souvenir or gift.

Along the 18km (11¼ miles) to **El Bosque** the road goes through a stunningly beautiful mountain landscape. Above 1,000m (3,281ft) there are pinsapo firs which occur naturally nowhere else in Eu-

*View from the south-east towards Grazalema*

*The landscape around El Bosque*

rope. In other parts are pines, cork oaks, almonds, olives, carobs, poplars and eucalyptus. Past the hamlet of Benamahoma the road descends more steeply to reach a junction where you go right towards El Bosque. Note the Los Nogales municipal swimming pool on the left if it's hot and you want a dip.

Trout farming in fresh mountain water is a big activity in **El Bosque**. Not surprisingly its mini-parador, much like Grazalema's is called Hostal Las Truchas (tel: 56-71 60 61). Again, pick up information on hiking and horse riding from the information centre (next to the municipal pool).

It is 16km (10 miles) along a mountainous road to Ubrique. Streams fill the Embalse de los Hurones on the right. About halfway along, the ruins of the Castillo de Tavizna rise up on the left. One would not expect many of isolated **Ubrique**'s 18,000 inhabitants to know of Dior and other famous fashion houses but they do. The town's workshops make elegant leatherware and accessories for top labels. Rumour has it that some workshops attach pirate labels. *Piel de Ubrique* is good-quality leather from which factories or family workshops make well-designed products. You can see them doing so and you'll probably be tempted to buy their handiwork.

If it's time for lunch, select a place in town or stop at the **Venta**

*Pigs among the cork oaks*

**el Chorizo** on the road to Cortes to sample its choice of sausages. Small and lonely **Cortes de la Frontera** is 25km (15½ miles) away along a road which goes through more spectacular mountain scenery, with Los Pinos peak on the left rising to almost 1,400m (4,593ft). You pass through parts of a hunting reserve, supposedly abundant in deer. Through Cortes head for Ronda with the Río Guadiaro on the right and 10km (6¼ miles) away is the **Cueva de la Pileta**.

The cave was discovered in 1905 by local farmer José Bullón and, after Altamira in Cantabria, is said to contain the most important examples of cave painting in Spain. If you wait by your car one of José's descendants will come along to lead you into the cave by the light of an oil lamp. Palaeolithic man used these caverns carved by an underground river and amid the stalagmites and stalactites left numerous traces of his habitation. With charcoal, yellow and red ochre paintings on the walls, early man depicted some of the things around him.

From Pileta, backtrack for 3km (1¾ miles) and go left, then through the hamlet of Jimera de Líbar and right on the c341 to Gaucín. The road is on a ridge between the Guadiaro and Genal rivers and affords grand views on its way through the villages of Benadalid and Algatocín. From **Gaucín** follow *Pick & Mix* Itinerary 5 in reverse to **Casares** back to Marbella (in Gaucín, take the Centro Ciudad road by the petrol station, then take the first right, which is unsignposted).

## 11. Roman Arcos, Traditional Villages and Windsurfing

**Monumental town, Roman ruins, breathtakingly beautiful mountain scenery, white villages, into Cádiz province, along the Ruta del Toro, the Atlantic coast, windsurfing paradise.**

Follow the Day 3 Itinerary to **Ronda** and then *Pick & Mix* Itinerary 10 as far as **Grazalema** (see overnight stops in itinerary 11) and **El Bosque**. Make an early start after the overnight stop and take the c344 road to **Arcos de la Frontera** through undulating agricultural land much of which is ablaze with extensive fields of sunflowers in June and July. After some 30km (18¾ miles) the outline of Arcos stretched atop a crag appears across the waters of its lake. Follow signs to the town centre and park before entering the narrow, rising street to the **Conjunto Historico**. Arcos is on the much-promoted *pueblos blancos* ('white towns') route and gets a lot of visitors.

To the Romans this was Arcobriga;

*Arcos de la Frontera*

the Moors named it Medina Arkosh and, after taking it in 1264, the Christians called it Arcos 'of the frontier'. The main square, from which there are extensive views across the Río Guadalete valley, is dominated by the Platersque façade of the **Iglesia de Santa María**. The church is of Visigothic origin but was built mainly between the 16th and 18th centuries. Inside are a notable baroque choir by Roldán and paintings by Alonso Cano. Also on the *plaza* are the Parador Nacional (previously the Casa del Corregidor) and the Ayuntamiento. Nearby is the Gothic Iglesia de San Pedro with a handsome portico. Zurbarán, Pacheco and Ribera contributed to the altar paintings. There are several attractive restaurants hereabouts, including El Convento opposite the comfortable Hotel Marques de Torresota (2-star), on Callejon de las Monjas.

*Arcos de la Frontera*

Take the N342 (Cádiz) road from Arcos and very soon turn left on to the C343 signposted Paterna. Looking back, Arcos shows itself from a different side. The road passes through undulating fields of cereals, sunflowers and beets. A sign indicates that you are on the '**Ruta del Toro**', for it is indeed bull-raising country as the specially fenced areas indicate. Where the cattle graze white egrets are plentiful. Trees are bent to the northwest and in places eucalyptus trees shield fields from the prevailing winds.

After **Medina Sidonia**, another *pueblo blanco,* there is a high view over the agricultural plain through which you pass to reach yet another high-perched white town, **Vejer de la Frontera**, where modernity has not been allowed to make many

*Zahara beach*

inroads. From Vejer take the N340 (Cádiz) road and go left for a scenic 16-km (10-mile) drive to **Los Caños de Meca**, making a short detour if you like to **Cabo de Trafalgar**, off which Admiral Nelson defeated the Franco-Spanish fleet in 1805 but was mortally wounded. Nudists enjoy the lovely pine-backed beaches of **Los Caños**. A small road leads down through the thick pine woods to Barbate which has nothing of interest except in spring and early summer when boats bring in bloody loads of tuna killed offshore.

Passing marshlands and a string of simple eating places specialising in fish, the road goes through a military zone where long-horned cattle graze close to the Atlantic shore and then turns right over a bridge to **Zahara de los Atunes**, which lives off fishing, mostly tuna, and summer tourism. A magnificent sandy beach stretches south and in front of the luxury residential development of **Atlanterra**, which is much favoured by Germans (El Varadero *pensión* offers comfortable rooms next to the beach). From Zahara it is 11km (6¾ miles) to the N340 (Tarifa) road through rolling countryside in which I have seen a wonderful roadside display of wild flowers and grasses. On the road south keep an eye open for bulls on the surrounding hills. Some 15km (9¼ miles) on at the Hostal San José del Valle is the turn-off for an 8-km (5-mile) detour to the Roman ruins of **Bolonia** (closed on Sunday afternoon and all day Monday), or a little further on to a pretty bay and beach. Enquire at the bar near the ruins for permission to see the site.

Back on the N340 you are soon in windsurfers' paradise along the long and lovely **Los Lances** beach backed by pinewoods in which there are hotels, campsites, bars, eating places, windsurfing schools and specialist shops catering for the enthusiasts who throng to Europe's most highly rated and challenging place for the sport. Turn off right at **Camping Torre de la Peña II** to reach a typical windsurfing hang-out. Here with fanatics, and sometimes bored partners, you can relax over refreshments or a simple meal.

*Tarifa beach*

Winter winds from the southwest or northeast can reach up to 120kph (75mph) and the average annual wind speed in **Tarifa**, Europe's windiest place, is 34kph (21mph). Incessant wind is supposed to affect a person's mental balance and one wonders how the locals stay sane. Or do they? Perhaps it was a very windy day in 1294 when Gúzman el Bueno (the Good) offered to sacrifice five of his sons to the Moors rather than surrender the town. A Christian traitor had taken Gúzman's eldest son hostage for the Moors, who offered to hand him back if the town was surrendered. From the castle walls Gúzman threw down his own dagger saying 'Let my son be killed with an honourable weapon.' The son was killed, the town relieved by Christian reinforcements and Gúzman rewarded with large tracts of land and honours which included the founding of the aristocratic Medina Sidonia line; at present the holder of the title is an erudite, left-wing campaigning duchess.

Tarifa is a characterful and attractive town, a world apart from the resorts east of Algeciras. Windsurfing has enlivened the narrow streets with interesting shops, bars, eating places and tanned and athletic young people. If you want to absorb more of its pleasant

*Tarifa, Europe's windiest place*

ambience than passing through allows, there are a number of small hotels. Inexpensive and recommended is Hostal-Restaurante El Asturiano, Calle Amador de los Ríos (tel 56-680619), where you can also get a very reasonable *menú del día*.

Ferry boats and hydrofoils ply to Tangier in North Africa, often visible across the Straits. Fortifications and the solid 10th-century castle, which is being restored, reflect the town's strategic importance.

You will probably want to drive as fast as you can through the industrial mess which surrounds Algeciras and through the port town itself. Across the bay is the **Rock of Gibraltar** with its egocentric community of some 30,000 people defying integration with Spain. From San Roque, where many Spaniards moved when Gibraltar became British, it is some 60km (37¼ miles) to Marbella.

## 12. Spa Cure, Salt Lake and Parador

**Take a 'cure' at mineral water spas (June to October); visit timeless villages, lakes, breeding grounds of flamingoes, monumental Antequera; stay overnight in its parador, and see the stark landscapes of El Torcal, the verdant views of the Montes de Málaga.**

(Telephone the **Parador de Antequera**, tel: 284 0061, to book a room for tonight.) Follow *Pick & Mix* Itineraries 2 and 6 as far as **Monda** and then take the MA413 and C344 via Guaro to Tolox. Don't go into the village of Tolox, stuck on a hillside, but bear left up a small valley to the **Balneario de Fuente Amargosa**. It is in a delightful riverside setting and its waters are supposed to be good for lung and kidney ailments.

Back to the C344 and at the village of Alozaina go left to Casarabonela and on through changing scenery to **Ardales** with a detour to **Carratraca** (see Itinerary 6). If you have been able to

take a plunge in the spa's waters, you should have done your respiratory system and skin some good. From Ardales go on to a junction and bear left to Teba on a road through agricultural lands. Teba (2km/1 mile) off the road) has an active leather industry and local shops have reasonably priced goods.

From Campillos, a lively agricultural town, also known for its leather (pick up picnic supplies, if you like, from the market next to the central church, with its massive Moorish doors), go north to sleepy Sierra de Yeguas and then right towards Fuente de Piedra (if you miss this small road – very easy – simply drive on to the Autovia and take the Málaga direction for 9km/5 miles). Just before the village turn right to the **Laguna de la Fuente de la Piedra** where there is a reception centre of AMA, Andalusia's environmental agency. In winter and spring (provided there isn't a drought), the observation area offers good views of the thousands of flamingoes on the largest salt lake in Spain. With the Camargue in France it is the last refuge in Europe where the greater flamingo nests. The mudflats all but dry up in summer but in spring have around 800mm (31½ inches) of water, a depth favoured by the flamingoes. Mallards, coots, black-headed gulls, owls, Montague's harriers and kestrels also take refuge here. Stilts and red-crested pochards nest here in summer; shovelers in winter. An old man toiling in the adjacent fields told me that during the Civil War hunger drove him to eat flamingo meat; it didn't taste good. He preferred the ducks but they weren't as numerous.

Take the road signposted **Antequera** and there follow signs to the **Parador**. Its pool will be a welcome sight if it's been a hot day, and its dining-room serves local specialities.

The next day follow the relevant part of the Day 4 Itinerary for sightseeing in Antequera and return to Marbella via **El Torcal** and the **Montes de Málaga**.

*Laguna de la Fuente de la Piedra*

# Shopping

**O**ver the years, I have done a lot of window-shopping in Marbella, your Costa del Sol base, and there has been much I have wanted to buy but could not afford. But, even if I had the money, I would probably do most of my shopping in Madrid or Barcelona where the prices are often lower than in Marbella. With less competition and a very high concentration of wealthy people as their clientele, Marbella's shopkeepers have been tempted to make premium mark-ups. Over the last two crisis high seasons many of them have complained to me about lack of custom; some have done a rethink about their marketing; some have closed down. All that said, Marbella – the town and Puerto Banús – has a good range of smart shops in which you can have a field day, or two, if paying more does not trouble you.

Generally, shops are more competitive in **Málaga**, where there is also an extensive choice, including **El Corte Inglés** department store (see Day 2). Torremolinos, especially appealing to younger tastes,

*Extravagant fashion in Puerto Banús…*

*...and Marbella*

and Fuengirola also offer a good and varied choice of shopping with a less exclusive image than Marbella and at generally lower prices (see Itineraries 8 & 9). Nerja, east of Málaga, is another resort town with a fair selection of good speciality outlets (Itinerary 7). And the choice is increasing in Estepona, especially for arts and crafts (Itinerary 3). There are branches of some fashion chains in all these locations. Inland too you should be on the look-out for interesting shops, more so for local arts and crafts and most notably in Benahavís (Day 1), where La Aldea offers some very stylish local products, including sculptures by David Marshall; Ronda (Day 3); Grazalema (Itinerary 10); Ubrique (Itinerary 10); Frigiliana; and Competa (Itinerary 7).

## Markets

Much to the indignation of Marbella's expensive boutique owners, everyone shops in the *mercadillos* these day, even the rich. Prices in the markets are unbeatable. For example: a cotton shirt, a copy of a designer original, for 2,000 pesetas; jeans for half the price of those found in a department store; the same with bath and beach towels; and toiletries at prices with which *droguerías* cannot compete; ceramic cookware much cheaper than any houseware or souvenir shop; nuts and sweets priced lower than at supermarkets; the list goes on.

**Markets** are held from 9am–2pm around Marbella football grounds on Monday, and on Thursday in San Pedro's Avenida Príncipe de Asturias. Especially good for arts and crafts is the Sunday *mercadillo* in Puerto de Estepona. The biggest market along the coast west of Málaga is around Fuengirola's bullring on Tuesday. It is acceptable to do some gentle bargaining but if you push your luck you may unleash a verbal torrent.

## Marbella's Shopping Areas

Shopping areas are located throughout Marbella's **Old Town**; on Avenida Ramón y Cajal opposite the Parque de la Alameda, and at the Marbella Centre at the avenue's eastern end; along Avenida Miguel Cano and the streets west of it, including Calle Alonso Bazán; the whole length of Avenida de Ricardo Soriano; Puerto Banús, including the adjoining Benabola and Gray d'Albion centres; also at the nearby Christamar complex; Nueva Andalucía's Centro Plaza; San Pedro de Alcántara – and on the streets east of Calle Marqués del Duero (the main street).

**Small arcades** in some of the **top hotels** have boutiques with a select range, mostly high-fashion clothing and accessories. There are also shops, especially good for home decoration buys, in commercial centres lining the N340.

## What to Buy

### Antiques

Silver and gold work, religious paintings and statues, carved and gilt picture and mirror frames, ceramic tiles, water pitchers and washing bowls, handmade glass, embossed copperware, embroidered cloth, fine lace, furniture with intricate inlay work and rustic furniture are among the things to buy. **El Rastro de Río Verde** (N340 km176) is a big emporium – with everything from knicknacks to huge things needing a truck for transport – where it is still possible to make good finds. In Marbella town, scout around El Arte de Giles, Edificio Marbelsun and Calle Jacinto Benavente. An **antiques market** is held on Saturday morning near the bullring in Nueva Andalucía. Rarer finds and better buys are often made in hole-in-the-wall shops in inland villages and towns. And this may also be possible in weekly *mercadillos* when stallholders may not be aware of the value of something old they have.

### Art

You are unlikely to find art in Marbella's galleries which, over the years, will prove to be an exceptionally good investment unless there is a special exhibition of works for sale by Antonio López, Antoni Tàpies, Miguel Barceló or other names among Spain's *firmas consagradas* (hallowed signatures). But there is a lot of good art to be seen on permanent exhibition and at special showings in the town's art galleries and top hotels. Three good galleries to begin

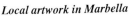

*Local artwork in Marbella*

with are: **Manuela Vilches**, Centro Comercial Marbella Real (N340 km179); **Llamas**, Avenida Ricardo Soriano 49; **Van Gestel**, Plaza de los Naranjos. The tourist office can provide a list of painters and sculptors resident in the town.

### Crafts

**Ceramics** top the list. There are traditional utility and decorative items and imaginative new shapes and designs. They are roughly or finely formed, glazed or unglazed, garishly coloured or finely painted. Pieces range from a souvenir ashtray or vase to a full dinner service from the renowned **Cartuja de Sevilla** factory. Ceramic shops are everywhere and don't forget the markets.

**Designer items** for home decoration by Spain's new wave of creative talent can be found in many different media from papier-maché to glass and metals and these can be ideal mementoes or gifts. **Esparto** and other grasses are woven to make many items which can also be good buys. Baskets are of all sizes and shapes for decoration or daily use. Other items include table mats, lampshades, painted wallhangings, picture and mirror frames, and all shapes of small boxes and slippers. **Bamboo** is used to make small containers, handbags, furniture of all sizes, screens and blinds.

Fans, shawls, *mantillas*, decorative haircombs: **traditional dress** accessories of Andalusian women can be lasting mementoes of your visit and unusual gifts. There is a great variation in quality and the best is not usually found in souvenir shops but in speciality shops used by local women. **Guitars** and **castanets** are good buys if you have a musical bent. **Leather** is no longer so much cheaper in Spain. Look for small workshops selling handcrafted items of their own design. The best buys of a range of leather goods can be made direct from factories in Ubrique and Teba and Campillos (Itinerary 12). Woodcarvings of good craftmanship are not widely found but in Marbella **Ricardo Dá Vila** does very fine work in olivewood at his small *taller*, Calle Caballeros 21, where he can be seen at work. What's good to see is that Ricardo is teaching his craft to a young apprentice.

## Fashion

My earlier remarks about higher prices are most pertinent in respect of fashion shopping. Generally, I find that clothes of comparable quality are more expensive in Spain than in the United States or in other parts of Europe – and in Marbella even more so. The fashion clothes and accessory shops are concentrated in the places listed under 'Marbella's Shopping Areas' above.

You will find shops with international names like Gucci and Benetton but my best advice for fashion clothing, jewellery and other accessories is to go for the labels of the big crop of very talented designers who have flowered in recent years to put Spain in the limelight of the fashion world. Just 10 names among Spain's **leading designers** are: Adolfo Domínguez, Jesús del Pozo, Manuel Piña, Sybilla, Purificación García, Roser Mercé, José Tomas, Toni Miró, Pedro Moreno and Vitorio y Luchino.

*Souvenir flamenco dolls*

# Eating Out

Local specialities tend to be fairly basic dishes that can be excellent if the ingredients are good. *Gazpacho* is a subtle blend of oil, vinegar, tomatoes, cucumbers, onions and stale bread dished up as a wholesome cold soup; *sopa ajo blanco con uvas* is something similar made with garlic, almonds and grapes; a good *paella* combines fresh morsels from the sea with available pieces of chicken and pork, a sprinkling of vegetables and a base of rice; *cocido* is like a peasant hotpot found in many countries in which what's available is all cooked together – meats, chicken, ham bone, sausages, vegetables, dried beans and lentils, potatoes – to make two courses of a soup served with rice or noodles followed by the meats and vegetables; the much-lauded *fritura malagueña* is in practice nothing more than a mixed fish fry which is only delicious when the fish is very fresh and the fryer contrived to get the oil at just the right temperature.

In recent years a number of factors have combined to bring about a culinary revolution in Andalusia. Meats of much better quality have become available; improved agricultural management has yielded better-quality vegetables and fruits, and new varieties, including tropical fruits, have been introduced. There are more well-trained chefs, too; there is a new interest in looking back to Arab times for inspiration, in refining other traditional dishes and in creating new ones in line with the modern Mediterranean style of lighter, healthier cooking. With affluence has come a new perception about food as being more than a necessary stomach-filler. Nowhere more so than in Marbella has the need to satisfy sophisticated international tastes raised standards.

## Tapas

It has long been the custom in bars to cover (*tapar*) glasses with small plates – perhaps, originally, to keep flies out of the wine or beer. The idea evolved to put titbits of food on these plates, perhaps to help soak up alcohol so customers would drink more. The cooked combinations, usually served warm, dis-

*La Hacienda in Urbanización Hacienda de Las Chapas*

play the most inventiveness. Just a few of these you might try are kidneys in sherry sauce, octopus diced with tomato and garlic, rabbit in almond sauce, lamb stews, crisply fried fish, prawns, mussels and other shellfish plain or with complementary sauces, battered and fried peppers and other vegetables. *Serrano*, ham which is salt-cured and dried in the high mountain air, is both a popular *tapas* and an ingredient in other dishes. The best comes from Jabugo in Huelva province and Treveléz in Granada's Sierra Nevada. *Tapas* are usually displayed under glass on a counter and prices are often indicated on a blackboard, so they are easy to order.

## Wine

The sherries from Cádiz province have for long been the most important Spanish wines in terms of international prestige and exports. Málaga's lusciously sweet and heavy dessert wine was a special favourite of the British and is making a comeback. Córdoba's Montilla-Moriles area also produces *vinos generosos* with much of its production shipped to Jerez to be bottled as sherries. Increasingly, Córdoba as well as Cádiz and Huelva provinces are producing crisp and light white table wines. Villages throughout Andalusia produce for local consumption their own *vino de terreno* which usually has quite a kick. You should cautiously sample it in villages like Manilva, Competa and Frigiliana.

## Shopping for Foodstuffs

Meat, fish, vegetables, fruit: mornings, daily except Sunday and holidays in the *mercados* of Marbella and San Pedro. Wines and liquors: Casa Pablo, C Gómez de la Serna. All provisions: Hiper Marbella, N340 west of town.

79

## Recommended dining in Marbella

Recommendations have been made in the Day and *Pick & Mix* Itineraries, and include the following places which I do not think you should miss: **La Fonda** in Marbella Old Town (Day 1); **La Hacienda** in Urbanización Hacienda Las Chapas (Day 2); **La Meridiana** in Urbanización Las Lomas de Marbella (Day 3); **beach clubs** of Hotels Don Carlos, Los Monteros, Marbella Club or Puente Romano for a buffet lunch (Day 5); **Marbella Club Restaurant Grill** (Day 5). And in the countryside: **El Coto** (Day 3) **Refugio de Juanar** (*Pick & Mix 2*). A few more restaurants are included among my top recommendations. I must admit, though, I have not eaten in all of Marbella's more than 200 restaurants.

## The Best

GRAN MARISQUERIA SANTIAGO
*Avenida Duque de Ahumada 50*
*Tel: 277 4339*
This is by far the best of the many restaurants along Marbella's seafront. As the name implies, seafood is the speciality and there is a concentration on its quality, careful preparation and refined service.

GITANJLI MAYFAIR
*N340 km179 (next to Aresbank)*
*Tel: 282 1519*
A new and sumptuous Indian restaurant where mention of the word 'curry' will raise the ire of the formidable host, Mr Jetty Singh, to a highly spiced heat. His personally created and extravagantly described dishes are evocations in taste and presentation of the sort of foods Mr Singh's father used to serve guests at the hunting lodge on his Punjabi estate. A special corner is devoted to the memory of the late Peter Sellers, a close friend, who without doubt copied Mr Singh's accent for the song *Goodness Gracious Me* which he sang to Sophia Loren.

EL PUENTE
*Hotel Puente Romano*
*N340 km177–8. Tel: 277 0100*
Especially recommended for summertime dining on its terrace overlooking the small Roman bridge. Simón Padilla has added his own creative dishes to a selection of Spanish and international favourites. The professional staff is attentive but it would be nice if they smiled more.

## La Dorada
*N340 km176*
*(near Coral Beach Hotel)*
*Tel: 276 2333*
Nautical ambience with fish and sea-food of the highest quality. Part of a small chain which has its own fishing boats to service the demands of this and its other prestigious restaurants in Madrid, Barcelona and Seville.

## Don Leone
*Muelle Ribera 45, Puerto Banús*
*Tel: 281 4962*
Freshly made pasta dishes and other Italian favourites to enjoy on a summertime terrace, or indoors, at the centre of it all along the wharf.

## The Rest
### Chinese

## Hong Kong
*Edificio Esperanza*
*Avenida Duque de Ahumada*
*Tel: 282 2003*
Basic décor, all the usual Cantonese dishes and charming service.

### Italian

## Toni Dalli
*Tel: 277 0035*
Famous Marbella institution run by ex-opera singer. Live Music most evenings. Sometimes Toni Dalli performs himself.

## Casa Nostra
*Calle Camilo José Cela 12*
*Tel: 282 7371*
Popular and efficiently run pizzeria serving good home-made pastas and grilled meats.

### International

**Mesón Raul** (Calle de los Caballeros); **El Patio** (Calle Buitrago); **Balcón de Virgen** (Calle Ortiz de Molinillo) and **Restaurante Mena** (Plaza de los Naranjos) are four places unlikely to disappoint and prices are moderate.

### Spanish

## Triana
*Calle Gloria*
*Tel: 277 9962*
Specialises in Catalan dishes. Reasonable prices.

## Bar Altamirano
*Plaza Altamirano*
A very popular bar, especially among locals who come for its good value seafood and bustling ambience.

Unpretentious eateries in the Old Town (See Day 1) where you can sample tasty food at reasonable prices include **Vinacoteca Riojana** (Calle Mesoncillo or Peral 8); **Restaurante Sol y Sombra** (Calle Tetuán 7); **Bar Ceuta** (Calle Buitrago).

# Calendar of Special Events

Whenever you come to the Costa del Sol, but especially during the summer, there is likely to be the opportunity to witness or participate in a *fiesta*, *feria* or *romería*. To find out what special events are happening during your visit, call in at the local tourist office when you arrive.

A *fiesta* usually has a religious connotation, such as the celebration of a saint's day, and the night before there is often a *verbena* of music and dancing in the open air. Revered images on *pasos* (floats) are carried in procession through the streets and there is often an open air Mass.

*Romerías* are pilgrimages in brightly decorated wagons and cars, on horseback and on foot to a permanent or temporary religious shrine in the countryside. There is an earthiness to both *ferias* and *romerías*, an explosion of merrymaking when the religious ritual has been observed.

*Ferias* have more to do with a village or town's cel celebration of itself, another reason for a week-long communal party. The people stop work, and show off in traditional costume, parade on fine horses, spend time at *corridas*, singing and dancing *flamenco*, listen to Spanish singing stars and rock-flamenco groups, eat a lot in specially-built *casetas* and consume litres of free-flowing *vino de terreno*. Noise is a common denominator of all these celebrations and fireworks displays are the climax of many.

*Verdiales* are Málaga province's own form of folk expression: music, Moorish in origin, is made by groups called *pandas* whose members wear brightly decorated straw hats, on an assortment of instruments. On 28 December they compete in a grand get-together at the Venta de San Cayetano, Puerto de la Torre near Málaga city.

## JANUARY

**Cabalgate de los Reyes** (6th), float parades of the Three Kings distributing sweets. This is the date for giving 'Christmas' presents to children.

There are a number of saints' feast days in January, including St Anthony in Mijas and Nerja, and St Sebastian in Casabermeja. Consult the tourist offices for exact dates.

*Semana Santa*

## FEBRUARY

**Carnaval**, banned under Franco, has been revived as a pre-Lenten outburst of indulgence.

## MARCH / APRIL

**Semana Santa** (Easter Week) is the time when Spain returns to the Dark Ages. Images of the Virgin and Christ are carried on richly ornate *pasos* by members of *cofradías* (brotherhoods). Hooded *nazarenos* walk ahead. Only shuffling feet, tinkling bells, muffled drums and the occasional *saeta* (song of devotion and praise) break the silence and thousands of candles light the darkness. Each village and town has its own procession and Seville's *Feria de Abril* (starting on the 18th unless it conflicts with Easter) is Spain's most exuberant spring festival: it is worth making a special visit to Seville (see *Insight Pocket Guide: Seville, Córdoba and Granada,* a companion guide to this one).

## MAY

**Cruces de Mayo** (3rd) has neighbourhoods competing with crosses decorated with paper flowers while children re-enact the *Semana Santa* (holy week).
**Corpus Christi** (can be in June) sees more processions along streets covered with petals and herbs.

## JUNE

In the week of the 11th Marbella celebrates its *Fiesta de San Bernabé* when a procession of Moors and Christians commemorates the town's recapture by the Catholic kings.
**Día de San Juan** (23rd) is a national day of recovery after celebrations the previous night around bonfires on which effigies of Judas are burned at the stake with displays of fireworks.
**Virgen del Carmen** (16th), the Patroness of fishermen, is honoured by processions of boats. Those in Estepona, Málaga and Nerja are among the biggest.

## AUGUST

**Feria de Málaga**, celebrated during the first fortnight, emulates Seville's Spring Fair. Marbella immediately follows with its week-long *Fiestas del Sol* which is on a smaller scale.

## SEPTEMBER

**Feria y Fiesta de Pedro Romero** (first fortnight), plus bullfighting, including the *Corrida Goyesca* in early 19th-century costumes.

## OCTOBER

**Feria y Romería del Rosario**. In the first full week, Fuengirola has a big *feria* and a *romería* to a field off the N340 where the Virgin's shrine is a brightly-dressed, covered wagon. In San Pedro de Alcántara, its saint's day on the 19th is marked by an open air Mass and a procession. Mijas has a pilgrimage at the end of October.

# PRACTICAL information

## BEFORE YOU GO

### Orientation

Marbella stretches for 26km (16 miles) along Spain's Costa del Sol in the province of Málaga which is one of Andalusia's eight provinces. Andalusia is one of Spain's 17 Autonomous Communities and Seville is its capital. Marbella's resident population is around 80,000.

Málaga city, the provincial capital, has over half a million inhabitants. The dual carriageway N340 (E15) coastal highway runs westwards from Málaga for 56km (34¾ miles) to Marbella, passing Málaga airport some 7km (4¼ miles) from the city centre. Seville is 220km (136¾ miles) northwest from Málaga along a new highway; Córdoba is 185km (115 miles) north; Granada is 130km (80¾ miles) to the northeast.

In time, Spain is in line with the majority countries of continental Europe: in summer two hours ahead of GMT; in winter one hour ahead.

Andalusians speak Castilian with some variations. If you don't speak the language, buy one of many good phrase books available.

Telephone codes for Andalusia's provinces are: Málaga (all Marbella numbers) 95; Seville 95; Córdoba 957; Granada 958; Cádiz 956; Huelva 959; Almería 950; Jaén 953. Drop the 9 when dialling from abroad and first add 34, the code for Spain.

### Climate and Clothing

The Costa del Sol has a typically Mediterranean climate which means hot summers, most rainfall during relatively mild winters, equitable and agreeable spring and autumn weather. The Sierra Blanca backing Marbella gives it a microclimate, a little cooler than most of the south coast and a little warmer in winter. The average temperature is 18°C (64°F) with an average of 320 days of sunshine. In summer temperatures may exceed 30°C (86°F) and in winter rarely go below 12°C (54°F). All that said, there have been contradictory weather patterns over the last few years. January temperatures in 1995, for example, were similar to those of late spring, and were accompanied by a severe drought that led to water rationing.

Loose-fitting cotton clothing is the obvious choice for summer; add some light sweaters for spring and autumn; things a little heavier and a light raincoat and umbrella for winter. Marbella is a fashion-conscious place but the style is casual.

### When to Go

Any time. The main season for visitors, when most places servicing them are in full swing, is from mid-June to end-September. In winter, however, you will find bargain car hire and accommodation. If you are a golfer, winter is probably the most attractive season; nature-lovers should not miss nature's glorious springtime display in Andalusia.

## GETTING THERE

### By Air

Flying to Málaga airport on scheduled or charter services, with or without an accommodation 'package', is the most popular way. The airport's capacity has recently being doubled to 11 million passengers per year and there are many more inter-continental services. Seville and Jerez de la Frontera are other points of arrival by air. Gibraltar is another.

Travel agents will have the latest information on availability of flights and packages. Málaga has all the usual facilities of a Grade 1 international airport, including excellent duty-free shopping. There is a regular bus service to Marbella. Check the current taxi fare to Marbella at the information desk before leaving the airport; take only registered taxis and discuss the fare in advance.

### By Road

Drivers head for Málaga and then Marbella along Spain's fast improving road network. Soon they will speed from

Rome, Copenhagen or London without being stopped by lights (but perhaps, still, by a highway patrolman). Consult with motoring organisations in your country.

### By Rail

Málaga is also the Costa del Sol's main rail terminus (tel: 231 2500) and again extensive infrastructural improvements in the network have improved and speeded up services. RENFE is the national rail operator and its *talgo* trains are the best. Travel agents can provide information about routes, times and fare schemes.

### By Sea

Cruise liners regularly call at Málaga and a scheduled service by Trasmediterránea connects with Barcelona and the Canary Islands.

Marbella's three marinas are at: Puerto Banús (tel: 281 4750); Puerto de Marbella (tel: 277 5700) and Puerto Cabo Pino (tel: 283 1975).

### Documents

Everybody requires a valid passport to pass into Spain. Citizens of other European Community countries and some countries such as the United

States and many Latin American states do not need visas for stays of up to 90 days. Consult the Spanish Consulate in your country before departure. Medical certificates are not required of people arriving from most parts of the world. Driving licences issued in the EU are valid, visitors from outside the EU need an International Driver's Permit.

### Customs Regulations

These are generally in line with other EU countries. Airlines, travel agents, and the Spanish Tourist Office and Consulate can advise.

### Electricity

220 Volts AC through two-pin round plugs. Bathrooms and a few older buildings may have a 110 Volt supply. Adaptors are widely available.

## MONEY MATTERS

Yes, you do need it, and quite a lot to enjoy the best of life on the Costa del Sol. The peseta is issued in 10,000, 5,000, 2,000 and 1,000 notes and 500, 200, 100, 50, 25, 10, five and one coins. Coins of 25 and 100 pesetas are the most useful for parking meters,

telephones and slot machines.

All major credit and charge cards are accepted, Visa most widely. And there are many cashpoints at which credit cards can be used with PINs.

Banks, which are plentiful, are the best places to exchange currency. They are open Monday–Friday from 8.30am –2pm and Saturday until 1pm. Most are not open on Saturday from June to September. Exchange booths are open longer hours. They offer a poorer rate of exchange, but often don't charge commission.

### Tax

IVA, a value-added tax, applies on most goods and services at the rate of 6 per cent and 12 per cent on goods and services considered luxuries, such as top hotels, car hire and photo film, rising to 33 per cent on some others, such as furs and jewellery.

If you are making a large purchase and are a non-resident of Spain, ask about exemption from IVA but bear in mind you may then have to pay value-added tax in your own country.

## ACCOMMODATION

Hotels are officially rated from one to five stars with five stars plus *Gran Lujo* as the top rating. *Hostals* have one to three stars. *Pensións* have one or two stars. Officially classified Tourist Apartments (ATS) have one to three keys. Much of the accommodation in villas and apartments is unclassified. Tourist offices can give you current rates.

Travel pages of newspapers in your country will have advertisements for private lettings as well as advertisements by specialist villa and apartment holiday operators.

As I have said before, Marbella has an exceptionally good range of top-rated hotels. There is not space to give details of them all but I have singled out three as being rather special:

### The Best Hotels

MARBELLA CLUB HOTEL
*N340, km178.2*
*Tel: 292 2211*
Prince Hohenlohe retains a 25 per cent stake in his creation which still has

*Marbella Club Hotel*

surrounded by luxuriant trees, shrubs, flowers and lawns tended by a team of 28 gardeners. Directly accessible accommodation for 390 guests is luxuriously appointed, some exceptionally so, and is especially spacious. The El Puente and La Plaza restaurants overlook the gardens and the small Roman bridge from which the hotel took its name. Light meals are served around one of the two pools. The beach club restaurant specialises in an extravagant buffet lunch. In addition, there are two games rooms and Manolo Santana's Tennis Club; the hotel has arrangements with three golf clubs. $$$$$

*Manolo Santana*

the feel of an exclusive club for its 170 guests. Most of the staff have been around for a long time and it is evident that they are proud to be part of the place. Suites, bungalows and rooms, all luxuriously appointed, are spread out in a sub-tropical garden. Room service may be a bit slow because of the distance but you have added privacy. Public rooms are cosily luxurious; two restaurants meet high international standards; two freshwater pools, one heated, are never crowded; one is at the beach club which also has a fitness centre; arrangments for a choice of sports are easily made. The best Marbella and the Costa del Sol can offer. $$$$

## HOTEL PUENTE ROMANO
*(Gran Lujo)*
*N340, km177.7*
*Tel: 282 0900*
The 'Prince of Marbella' was also the originator of this larger complex where three-storey *pueblo*-style buildings are

## HOTEL LOS MONTEROS
*(Gran Lujo)*
*N340, km187*
*Tel: 277 1700*
Active, multi-sport enthusiasts cannot have it better: the beautiful Río Real Golf course is part of the offer; the Tennis Club has 10 courts and five squash courts (with more courts for both sports at the well-appointed Golf Club); Arabian horses await riders at the Club Hípico; at La Cabane Beach Club there are watersports. Up to 340 guests are accommodated in regionally decorated rooms within three pavilions surrounded by gardens which are graced by strutting flamingoes. There are two restaurants and light meals are served on the pool terrace. $$$$$

*Hotel Puente Romano*

## Other Recommendations

### $$$$$

**HOTEL DON CARLOS**
*N340, km192*
*Tel: 283 1140*
Two hundred and twenty-three rooms and 15 suites. Another of Marbella's classic hotels.

**HOTEL-SPA INCOSOL**
*N340, km184/5*
*Tel: 277 3700*
Comprising 197 rooms including suites. Fitness and medical centre.

**HOTEL CORAL BEACH**
*N340, km175*
*Tel: 282 4500*
This hotel has 170 rooms including suites. New, functional design.

### $$$$

**HOTEL EL FUERTE**
*Avenida El Fuerte.*
*Tel: 286 1500*
Including suites, 262 rooms. Central location, good facilities and well-run.

**GOLF HOTEL GUADALMINA**
*Hacienda Guadalmin*
*San Pedro de Alcántara*
*Tel: 288 2211*
Capacity for 180 in either rooms or bungalows.

### $$$

**HOTEL RINCON ANDALUZ**
*N340, km 173*
*Tel: 281 1517*

In a pretty *pueblo* development which has good amenities; 127 rooms.

**HOTEL LINA**
*Avenida Antonio Belon*
*Tel: 277 0500*
Town hotel. Good value. Rooms have bath and balcony.

### $$

**HOSTAL ENRIQUETA**
*Calle Los Caballeros*
*Tel: 282 7552*
Small, simple place very near to Plaza de los Naranjos. Closed in winter.

**PENSION EL CASTILLO**
*Plaza San Bernabé*
*Tel: 277 1739*
Basic but characterful and clean rooms for a predominantly young clientele. Good position.

## Three-Key ATs

**JARDINES DEL MAR**
*Paraje Don Pepe, to the west of town*
*Tel: 277 6000*
Comfortable two-room apartments in pleasant gardens.

**BENAVOLA PARK PLAZA**
*Puerto Banús*
*Tel: 281 5068*
Apartments for up to six people at the heart of the *puerto*.

## GETTING AROUND

## By Car

The biggest international car hire firms are represented in Marbella and at Málaga airport, but it may be cheaper to book before arriving in Spain. Some airlines have 'fly-drive' packages. In the travel pages of newspapers in your country there may be companies advertising budget car rentals and I have used some satisfactorily. Some 40 local

*The N340 coastal highway*

surance may give instructions and provide for special arrangements. You may need to get a *grua* (towing truck) and find a *taller* (repair shop). Motoring organisations in many countries have reciprocal arrangements with the Real Automovil Club de España, Plaza Uncibay 3, Málaga; tel: 221 4260.

*Gasolineras* (petrol stations) sell *normal* (92 octane), *super* (96), *gas-oil* (diesel) and, thankfully, more and more *sin plomo* (lead-free). Normal hours are 7am–10pm.

firms generally have better rates than the big operators. Two local firms to try are:

NIZA CAR INTERRENT
*Calle Alonso de Bazán, Marbella.*
*Tel: 277 0829*

RUAL
*N340, km178*
*San Pedro de Alcántara*
*Tel: 278 0408*

The rules of the road are much the same as in the rest of Western Europe but Spain suffers from a much higher than average road accident and death rate. Eccentric driving by locals and foreigners is a hazard.

The N340 is the main road along the coast. In areas along the road where fast vehicles could be a hazard speed is regulated by traffic lights which punctuate the road at regular intervals. If you travel too fast the next set of lights that you approach will turn red. If you find yourself going the wrong way along the N340, look for a *Cambio de Sentido*, where you can change your direction.

Car hire firms should tell you what to do in case of an accident or breakdown. If you are in your own car, your travel or car in-

## By Bus and Taxi

There are three urban bus routes in Marbella: Plaza de Toros through the centre to Hiper Marbella; Centre through Albarizas to Hotel Don Miguel; Centre to Club de Fútbol and to Miraflores. From the Bus Terminal on Avenida de Ricardo Soriano there is a spreading network of regular services along the Costa del Sol and to inland villages, towns and cities. The buses are comfortable and fares low.

Taxis are plentiful and relatively low-priced. Agree upon the fare in advance for longer journeys. There are fixed rates for most journeys. I make a mental or written note of the taxi's permit number in case I leave something in it or there is a dispute.

## COMMUNICATIONS AND MEDIA

### Keeping in Touch

Post Offices (*Correos*) are open from 9am–2pm Monday–Friday, 1pm on Saturday at Calle Alonso de Bazún 1, Marbella; tel: 277 2898, and Calle Hernán Cortés, San Pedro de Alcántara; tel: 278 0393.

To reach other countries by telephone from the Costa del Sol, first dial the international access code 07, then the relevant country code: Australia (61); France (33); Germany (49); Italy (39); Japan

## 19 MARBELLA

be a few supermarkets open as well as shops selling souvenirs, beach paraphernalia and the like.

## Public Holidays

In addition to local *fiesta* days and the changing dates for Easter and Whitsun, these are the public holidays in Andalusia:

| | |
|---|---|
| **1 January** | Año Nuevo |
| **6 January** | Día de los Reyes |
| **28 February** | Día de Andalucía |
| **19 March** | San José |
| **1 May** | Día del Trabajo |
| **24 June** | San Juan |
| **25 July** | Santiago (Spain's Patron Saint) |
| **15 August** | Asunción: |
| **12 October** | Hispanidad (Columbus' Day) |
| **1 November** | Todos los Santos |
| **8 December** | Immaculada Concepción |
| **25 December** | Navidad |

(81); Netherlands (31); United Kingdom (44); US and Canada (1). If you are using a US credit phone card, dial the company's access number below, then 01, and then the country code. Sprint, tel: 900 99 0013; AT&T, tel: 900 990011; MCI, tel: 900 99 0014.

## Media

*Sur*, Málaga's own daily newspaper in Spanish, publishes a free English edition every Friday. The monthly *Lookout* is the longest established English-language colour magazine in Spain. *Marbella Times* is a monthly society and advertising colour publication. *Die Aktuelle* gives good coverage of Costa del Sol matters in German. *La Costa Scanposten* does the same for Scandinavians. Billboards and leaflet handouts publicise special events as do hotels and sports clubs.

## HOURS AND HOLIDAYS

### Business Hours

Monday to Saturday from around 9/10am–1.30/2pm and again from between 4/5pm–8/9pm. Some shops do not reopen on Saturday afternoon; some supermarkets stay open later; so may department stores which also do not close for the *siesta*. On Sunday and public holidays there will usually

## EMERGENCIES

### Police

The *Policia Nacional* (tel: 091) deal with Spain's internal security and with law and order in the main urban areas. They have navy blue uniforms and their *comisaría* is in Calle Huerta Los Guerras (tel: 277 1193); regarding documents at Calle Portada 3 (tel: 277 4741) in Marbella.

The *Guardia Civil* look after law and order along the coastline, outlying urbanisations and in rural areas. They wear avocado green uniforms and their *cuartel* is at Plaza Leganitos in Marbella (tel: 277 1399), and Playa del Ancón, San Pedro de Alcántara (tel: 277 1944). They also run the highway patrol from Marbella's Calle San Antonio (tel: 277 2549).

The *Policia Local* (tel: 092), also in blue but with checked bands, are principally responsible for urban traffic

*A Cruz Roja first-aid post*

control and civil protection. Their offices are at the Ayuntamiento in Plaza de los Naranjos, Marbella (tel: 277 3194) and at Avenida Marqués del Duero 68, San Pedro de Alcántara (tel: 278 1262). They also deal with lost property at an office in Calle Serenata in Marbella (tel: 277 4349) and from the San Pedro office.

## Robbery

So much wealth attracts shady characters who rob from cars or private and hotel accommodation and make mugging attacks. The need to feed a drug dependence is the motivation for many, more so in cities like Málaga and Seville. I have not had any bad experiences in Marbella, but friends have. The best advice I can give is to take intelligent precautions, as you would anywhere, and not be ostentatious with money and jewellery.

## Accident and Sickness

If they have E110, E111 or E112 forms from their national health services, residents of EC countries benefit from reciprocal arrangements with SAS, Andalusia's public health service which, from my experience, is excellent. But I still recommend all short-term visitors to take out a Travel Insurance policy. The SAS Centro de Salud (Health Centre; Tel: 277 0245) is on Plaza Tetuán and a sparkling new general hospital is opening just east of the town.

Marbella has a very high population of *medicos* (doctors) in all the specialisations and a number of private clinics about which you can obtain local advice and recommendations. The

Marbella Clinic (tel: 277 4200) is on the town's eastern edge opposite the *gasolinera*.

Pharmacies (*Farmacias*) are identified by green or red crosses and can often advise and deal directly with minor ailments. Outside normal shopping hours they display the name and address of the nearest *farmacia de guardia* which will be open.

## Emergency Numbers

**Municipal Ambulance for Marbella**
 Tel: 277 0445
**Red Cross** *(Cruz Roja)*
 Tel: 277 4534/283 2929
**Private Services**
 Tel: 277 2526/277 2798
**Fire Brigade** *(Bomberos)*
 Tel: 277 4349

## SPORT

### Golf

Marbella has 11 courses and more are planned. Non-members can have difficulty in getting a game during peak periods (weekends and school holidays) or must settle for less convenient starting times, very early in the morning or in the highest heat of summer days. Premier hotels have arrangements for free access to certain courses but this does not necessarily help with booking a game at a convenient time. The best advice is to book a starting time well in advance through your hotel's concierge or direct with the club of your choice. High demand means that green fees are relatively high and these you can check out beforehand. And

remember that to play you need your handicap card from your home club.

All the clubs have professionals for coaching, offer golf clubs and cart rental and most have buggies for hire. All have a bar and restaurant and most have a swimming pool and tennis courts. Málaga's provincial tourist board publishes information. *Andalucía Golf* and *Costa Golf* are two informative local publications.

## Tennis

Wimbledon, Forest Hills and Roland Garros champion Manolo Santana's Tennis Club has the best facilities on the Costa del Sol and is very well run under Señor Santana's keen eye. There are five clay, four quick-surface and two artificial grass courts. Access is limited to guests of the Puente Romano and Marbella Club hotels, members of the tennis club and their guests. If you are a serious player it should not be too difficult to meet one of the club members and be invited for a game. An hour on a grass court costs around 4,000 pesetas (plus IVA) for non-members as against 1,800 for hotel guests. Annual membership for over-18s costs 82,500 pesetas and there are concessions for additional family members.

The club's coaching school has national recognition and lessons are available with a monitor or trainer. A well-equipped fitness centre also offers aerobics, yoga, sauna and massage. The Manolo Santana Tennis Club (tel: 277 0100) is on the west side of the growing Puente Romano complex.

*Marbella has 11 golf courses*

Another good venue on the other side of town is the Hotel Los Monteros Tennis Club (tel: 277 1700), where public access is easier although hotel guests have priority in booking courts. It has 10 quick-surface courts available at 1,400 pesetas (plus IVA) per hour. Lessons of 40 minutes cost 2,500 pesetas. Up in the hills 7km (4¼ miles) on the San Pedro to Ronda road, the El Madroñal Club de Campo (tel: 278 0990) is an informal place with a family atmosphere and has quick-surface courts available at 1,500 pesetas per hour. In the town the Hotel El Fuerte (tel: 277 1500) has good facilities. There are many more hotels with courts, including: Don Carlos, Marbella Dinamar, Estrella del Mar, Artola, Rincón Andaluz and Pinomar. And many of the golf clubs have tennis courts.

## USEFUL INFORMATION

The Municipal Tourist Office on Plaza de los Naranjos (tel: 282 3550) is open during normal business hours (see Day 1). In San Pedro de Alcántara the tourist office is located on Avenida Marqués del Duero (tel: 278 5252).

### Consulates (Consulados)

Many countries maintain local consulates, primarily in Málaga. Police, tourist offices and hotels can provide addresses and telephone numbers. A few are listed here:
Germany: 222 7866
Great Britain: 221 7571
USA: 247 4891

### Environment

Happily, this is now an urgent consideration for some people. If you have suggestions or complaints about environmental issues in the region call the *teléfono verde* (green phone) line on 277 4638.

## A

Abd-al-Rahman I 12, 17
Abd-al-Rahman III 13, 17
accidents 91
Acinipo 64
agriculture 12, 14, 33, 38, 47, 48, 50, 55
al-Andalus 12–14, 17
Al-Hafsun, Omar 56
Al-mansur 13
'alcazaba', 'alcázar' see castles
Alfonso XII 57
Alfonso XIII 17, 56
Algeciras 72
Algarrobo Costa 57
Alhambra (Granada) 14, 35
Almohades 14
Almoravides 14
Alora 55
Andalusia 10, 11, 15–16, 17, 84
Antequera 10, 11, 13, 15, 20, 38–42, 72
antiques 24, 76
aqueducts 11, 58
Arabs (see also Moors) 12, 45
architecture 12–13, 14, 15, 17, 23, 27, 28, 34–5, 39, 41, 42
Arcos de la Frontera 67–8
Ardales 55, 72
Arroyo de la Miel 30

## B

Baetica 11–12, 17
Ballesteros, Severiano 32
Barcelona 13, 17, 85
Basque country 12
beach clubs 43–4, 80
beaches 44, 58, 60, 69, 70
Benahavís 24, 75
Benalmádena 30, 60, 61
Berbers 12, 13
Boabdil 15
Bobastro 56
Bolonia 70
Bourbon dynasty 17
Bronze Age 17
bullfighting 30, 36, 50, 83
buses 85, 89
Byzantium 12

## C

Cabo de Trafalgar 70
Cádiz 11, 79
Cano, Alonso 17, 28, 68
Carlos V 17
Carratraca 55, 73
Carthaginians 10, 11, 17
Casabermeja 42
Casares 51–52, 67

Castellar de la Frontera 54
Castillo de Gibralfaro (Málaga) 28
castles 13, 21, 28, 29, 34, 39, 52, 53, 54, 55, 56, 66, 71
cathedrals 14, 15, 27
caves 39, 58, 67
Cela, Camilo José 24
Cervantes Saavedra, Miguel de 17
Christianity 12
churches 11, 23, 27, 28, 31, 39, 40, 41, 42, 50, 53, 55, 56, 68
'cocheros' 23
Coín 55
Columbus, Christopher 15, 16, 17
Competa 59, 75, 79
Córdoba 11, 12, 13, 14, 17, 56, 79, 84
Cortes de la Frontera 67
Costa Natura 51
Cueva de Menga 39
Cueva de Pileta 67
Cueva de Viera 39
Cuevas de Nerja 58

## D, E

Damascus 12
Degrain, Muñoz 28
Detunda 59
discos 45, 61
dolmens 10
earthquakes 57
El Bosque 65, 66, 67
El Chorro 56
El Madroñal 32
El Torcal 42
emergencies 90–1
Estepona 49–50, 75, 83
Expo '92 16, 17, 77, 85

## F

Felipe II 17, 36, 59
Felipe V 17
Ferdinand of Aragón 15, 41
Fernando VII 56
'fiestas' 59, 82–3

flamenco 25, 61, 63, 82
flamingoes 73, 87
fortifications 13, 15, 28, 71
Franco, Francisco 8, 17
Frigiliana 57, 59, 75, 79
Fuengirola 31, 62–3, 75, 83

## G

Gaucín 53, 67
Gibraltar 12, 33, 62, 72, 85
Gil, Jesús 9
Giralda Tower (Seville) 14
golf 32, 85, 85, 91–92
Gonzales, Felipe 17
Goya, Francisco 36
Granada 13, 14, 15, 17, 59, 84
Grazalema 64–5, 67, 75
Greeks 10–11, 17, 59
Gúzman el Bueno 53, 71

## H, I, J

Hadrian 12
Hakam II 13
Hapsburg dynasty 17
Hemingway, Ernest 30, 36
Hisham II 13
Hispano-Romans 12
Hohenlohe, Prince Alfonso von 16, 86
Iberians 10, 17
Infante, Blas 52
Isabella of Castile 15, 41
Islam 12
Istán 47–8, 49
Jerez de la Frontera 79, 85
Jews 12, 14, 15, 17
Jimena de la Frontera 54
Juan Carlos I 17, 56
Julius Caesar 11, 52

## L

La Aldea 22
La Axarquía 56, 59
Laguna de la Fuente de Pedra 72–3

Larios family 27, 30, 49
Las Navas de Tolosa (battle of) 14, 17
leather 66–7, 73, 77
León 13
Los Reales 51
Lucan 12

## M

Madrid 15, 17, 25
Mainake 59
Málaga 11, 13, 15, 18, 26–31, 38, 74,
    80, 83, 84, 85, 89
Málaga School 28
Malagueta, La (Málaga) 29
Manilva 52, 79
Marbella 8, 11, 13, 15, 16, 21–5, 75,
    76, 77, 78, 79, 80–1, 83, 84, 86–7,
    89, 90–1
Marbella Club 16, 23, 43, 44, 80, 86, 92
markets 27, 50, 51, 75, 76, 79
Martial 12
Medina Sidonia 68
Mena, Pedro de 27, 28
Mezquita (Cordóba) 14
Mijas 30–1, 62
Mohammed V 14
Monda 54, 72
Montes de Málaga 42, 73
Moors 12, 34, 39, 45, 47, 52, 53, 55, 57,
    62, 68, 71, 83
Morales, Luis de 28
'moriscos' 52
Moslems 12, 15
mudéjar style 14, 35, 41, 55, 56
Murillo, Bartolomé Esteban 17, 28
museums 11, 22, 27–8, 31, 41, 65

## N, O

Napoleon 17, 41
Nasrid dynasty 14, 15, 35
nature reserves 33, 42, 48, 49, 56, 73
Nerja 11, 57–8, 75, 83
night clubs 25, 45, 61, 63, 87
Nueva Andalucía 23, 75, 76

Ojén 48, 49, 54
Olympics 17
Ommayad dynasty 12, 19
Ossius 12

## P

Pacheco, Francisco 68
pharmacies 91
Phocaeans 10–11
Phoenicians 10, 11, 19, 55
Picasso, Pablo 28
Pompey 11
post office 89–90
prehistoric culture 10, 39, 58, 67
public holidays 90
Puente Romano (Marbella) 23, 42, 44, 80,
    87, 92
Puerto Banús 21, 23, 25, 37, 51, 75, 81,
    85, 88
Puerto Cabo Pino 31
Puerto de Benalmádena 60, 61
Puerto de Estepona 50, 51, 75
Puerto de las Pedrizas 38
Puerto de Sotogrande 54
Puerto Duquesa 52

## R

Reconquest 14–15, 83
Reformation 17
Refugio de Juanar 48–9, 80
Reserva Nacional de la Serranía de
    Ronda 33
Ribera, José de 28, 70
Río Genal 33, 53, 67
Río Guadalete 68
Río Guadalevín 34
Río Guadalhorce 55, 56
Río Guadalmedina 26
Río Guadalmina 24, 33
Río Guadiaro 33, 54, 67
Río Real 48
Río Verde 11
Rivera, Primo de 17
Roderick, King 17

Romans 11–12, 13, 17, 39, 55, 58–9, 68
'romerías' 47, 82–3
Romero, Pedro 36, 83
Ronda 15, 20, 32–7, 64, 75
Rueda, Salvador 30

## S

San Pedro de Alcántara 11, 21, 23, 24–5, 32, 75, 79, 83, 88, 90
Santana, Manolo 87, 92
Santiago de Compostela 13
Second Punic War 11, 17
Seneca 12
Serranía de Ronda 33, 48
Setenil 64
Seville 13, 14, 17, 83, 84, 85
shopping 25, 30, 57, 61, 74–7, 79, 90
Sierra Bermeja 50, 51
Sierra Blanca 46, 49, 84
Sierra de Aguas 55
Sierra de Alcaparain 55
Sierra Tejeda 59
Soriano, Don Ricardo 16
Spanish Civil War 17, 37
spas 55–6, 72, 73

## T, U

'taifas' 13–14
Tangier 71
'tapas' 78–9
Tarifa 53, 71

Tarik 17
Tartessos 17
telephones 84, 90
tennis 87, 92
theatres, Roman 11, 28, 64
Toledo 14
Torre del Mar 57
Torremolinos 60, 62, 74
Torrox Costa 57
tourism 9, 15–16, 17, 33
tourist information 22, 34, 49, 60, 74, 86, 88
Trajan 12
Ubrique 66, 75, 77

## V, W, Z

Vandals 17, 55
Vega, Lope de 17
Vejer de la Frontera 70
Velázquez, Diego Rodríguez 17
Vilanueva de la Concepcíon 42
vines 10, 52, 59
Visigoths 12, 13, 17, 68
War of the Spanish Succession 17
War of Independence 17
watersports 44, 87
Welles, Orson 36
wine 52, 59, 79
windsurfing 44, 70–1, 72
wrought iron 34–3
Zahara de los Atunes 69, 70
Zurbarán, Francisco de 28, 68

ACKNOWLEDGMENTS

*Photography by* **Jens Poulsen** *and*
*Pages 2–3, 8–9* **J D Dallet**

*Cover Design* **Klaus Geisler**
*Production Editor* **Gareth Walters**
*Handwriting* **V. Barl**
*Cartography* **Berndtson & Berndtson**